Richard Champion

Considerations on the present situation of Great Britain and the

United States of America

with a view to their future commercial connexions

Richard Champion

Considerations on the present situation of Great Britain and the United States of America
with a view to their future commercial connexions

ISBN/EAN: 9783742834300

Manufactured in Europe, USA, Canada, Australia, Japa

Cover: Foto ©knipser5 / pixelio.de

Manufactured and distributed by brebook publishing software
(www.brebook.com)

Richard Champion

Considerations on the present situation of Great Britain and the United States of America

CONSIDERATIONS

ON THE

PRESENT SITUATION

OF

GREAT BRITAIN

AND THE

UNITED STATES OF AMERICA,

WITH A VIEW TO THEIR FUTURE

COMMERCIAL CONNEXIONS.

CONTAINING

Remarks upon the Pamphlet publifhed by LORD SHEFFIELD, entitled,
" Obfervations on the Commerce of the American States ;" and alfo
on the Act of Navigation, fo far as it relates to thofe States. Inter-
fperfed with fome Obfervations upon the State of Canada, Nova Scotia,
and the Fifheries ; and upon the Connexion of the Weft Indies with
America : Together with various Accounts, neceffary to fhew the
State of the Trade and Shipping of both Countries.

THE SECOND EDITION, WITH GREAT ADDITIONS.

TO WHICH IS NOW FIRST ADDED,

The Plan of an Act of Parliament for the Eftablifhment and Regulation
of our Trade with the American States.

ALSO, A

PREFACE,

Containing Remarks upon the Authorities on which LORD SHEFFIELD
has formed the principal Part of his Obfervations.

BY RICHARD CHAMPION, Esq.

LATE DEPUTY PAYMASTER GENERAL OF HIS MAJESTY'S FORCES.

———— referent in mare te novi
Fluctus? O! quid agis? fortiter occupa
Portum————
———— tu, nifi ventis
Debes ludibrium, cave.

HOR.

LONDON:

PRINTED FOR JOHN STOCKDALE, OPPOSITE

BURLINGTON-HOUSE, PICCADILLY.

MDCCLXXXIV.

PREFACE.

THE Facts which are given to the World in the courfe of this Work, are of the moft public notoriety. The efficiency of them is the proper, and the only neceffary fupport. A Name of Confequence might give them brilliancy, but could not add to their own great and internal ftrength. A Name, therefore, without that Confequence, will not be productive of any benefit to them. Under this impreffion, the Author would certainly have again omitted his Name to this, as he did to the former Edition, had not other reafons been urgent with him to the contrary. Thefe were fuggefted, by obferving in Lord Sheffield's Treatife upon the Commerce of the American States, a ftrange perverfion of his Arguments, falfe deductions drawn from them, and even His words mifquoted. Compelled, therefore, to bring forward his Name to the Public, in defence of his Opinions, he submits to the necessity with humility and deference.

WHENEVER a Person is possessed of material information on any National Object, it is a duty which he owes to the Public, to communicate it to them. At this great and solemn period, when the most important Revolution perhaps ever known, has just passed; and under circumstances which, during their operation, menaced us in the most alarming manner, it would be a criminal negligence to with-hold any knowledge that might contribute to the happy settlement of our future connexions with the States of America; a settlement upon which our own welfare in so great a measure depends.

THE Author is charged in general terms, by Lord Sheffield, in page 7th of the Preface to the Observations which he has published, with arguing, that " the American States, " although now Foreign, ought to be indulged
" with

" with nearly all the Commercial Privileges
" and immunities which they enjoyed whilſt
" Britiſh Subjects—that, in return, they will
" ſupply our Weſt India Iſlands with Provi-
" ſions, &c. and take from them Sugar, Rum,"
&c. As far as the Author can comprehend
this charge, it appears to be founded upon
certain Facts, offenſive to the noble Writer,
though ſupported in general by our Commercial Intereſt, and in particular by a very great
and reſpectable part of it, the Weſt India Merchants and Planters. Speaking then generally
to it, the Author fully admits the charge, and
is prepared to juſtify the principle, upon this
ground; that the nearer approach we make to
the renewal of thoſe connexions, upon which the
grandeur of our Empire was founded, the nearer
approach we ſhall make to a Reſtoration of the
ſtate from which it has fallen. But the Author
never aſſerted, what the noble Lord is pleaſed
to aſſert for him, in the next page, viz. that the
Americans " will become our ſhip-builders,
" we being unable to build ſhips, and to
" Carry for ourſelves, but at an intolerable

a 2   " loſs."

" lofs." The Author afferted only, and he ftill afferts, that the Incorporation of American Shipping amongft ours, has been found, by long experience, to be of effential fervice to our Navigation; and that the continuation of this practice in future, in order to fupply the deficiencies, which we cannot procure to equal advantage elfewhere, will be the only means of preferving the Carrying Trade.

THE noble Lord further adds (fpeaking of this Work) " that this farther advantage is held " out to us, that the Americans will take our " Manufactures, when they cannot get the " fame articles cheaper, better, and on longer " credit, elfewhere." It is not furely a very inconfiderable advantage to have the preference of the cuftom of any Nation, when that Nation can procure them on equal terms from other places. The doctrinal Creed of a Man of Bufinefs is, to make his purchafes in the cheapeft markets, and upon the beft terms. And if America gives us the preference of purchafe, her connexion is beneficial to us. But, the
Author

Author is of opinion, judging from the difpofitions of thofe States upon the Peace to trade with us, that, with proper encouragement on our parts, their Commerce would, almoft exclufively, have fallen into our hands.

In the fame Preface to this laft Edition of the Obfervations on the Commerce of the American States, the noble Lord appears to be very inattentive to the Work that he undertook to criticife. For he has imputed words to the Author which are not to be found in his Work. Of thefe inftances the following are particularly material. Lord Sheffield, fpeaking of the former Edition of thefe Confiderations, has thefe words : " The article relative to Ame-
" rican fhipping, is the moft extraordinary of
" the whole ; he fays, 398,000 tons were em-
" ployed in the Commerce between Great
" Britain and America, exclufive of the Trade
" between the latter and the Weft Indies. The
" Author may eafily learn, that not 110,000
" tons were at any time employed in that
" Commerce."—In this obfervation, the paf-

fage

fage it refers to is wholly miftaken, and mifquoted. This appears by a reference to page
23 of the firft, and 32 of the prefent Edition of
thefe Confiderations, in which will be found
the words which Lord Sheffield has fo mifquoted, viz. " The American fhipping em-
" ployed in the Commerce of Great Britain
" (exclufive of the Trade between America
" and the Weft Indies) at the commencement
" of the American War, was 398,000 tons."
The noble Lord is the lefs excufable for this
miftake, as in page 24 of the firft, and 33 of
the prefent Edition, a diftinction is made, in
order to prevent " the confounding them with
" thofe fhips which carried on the Trade be-
" tween this Country and America."

THE Author will give the beft anfwer in
his power to the noble Lord's complaint,
which he makes in fuch loofe terms in page 7
of the Preface to the laft Edition of his Obfervations. This complaint is that " of 150 pages
" of this Work being filled with calculations
" and affertions, hazarded in the fame manner,
" without apparent authority." In the firft
Edition,

Edition, the Author faid, that the account of the fhips employed in the Commerce of Great Britain, was taken " from actual furveys of " the fhipping, and from evidence and papers " laid before Parliament;" and, in another place, that " there not being the fame regu♥ " larity in furveying the Trading veffels of " that Country (America) as is practifed in " Great Britain, and the Cuftom-houfe Books " not diftinguifhing the voyages which each fhip " made in the year, it is not poffible to give " fo very exact an account. But good infor- " mation, collected with care, and compared " with the produce of the different States, " very fully fupplies the deficiency." So far, therefore, the Author was not deficient in giving Authorities. Some indifputable, others the beft that could be procured. But as the noble Lord feems defirous of yet more parti- cular ones, and as, from his having miftaken what the Author has faid upon the fubject, it may be fuppofed, that he is not acquainted with that furvey of our fhipping from which the beft information is to be derived, the Au- thor now informs him, that the account of our

fhip

shipping, is taken from actual surveys, continually making, of the vessels trading to and from the different Ports of Great Britain. They contain the ship's name, that of the Masters, the place and the year in which she was built, the tonnage, the voyage which she has made, and the port in which she was surveyed. From this actual survey, the Author asserted, that at the commencement of the American War, there were, as nearly as could be ascertained, 398,000 tons of shipping, of the built of the Countries now composing the United Sates, employed in the general Commerce of Great Britain. *

In all that concerns the general principles of our Colonial Commerce, the Author has followed the opinions of Mr. Burke, whose great and comprehensive knowledge of that subject has produced an habitual deference to it. In the particular, as well as general parts, he has paid the strictest attention to those of Mr. Glover,

* The West India Planters and Merchants have given an account to the same purport, and from the same authority. It is not the exact number of ships, because the extracts were not probably made at the same identical period, the Books being corrected either weekly, or every fortnight; when the number of ships vary. The Author's extract was made from the Book dated 1775 and 1776.

Glover, whose judicious and accurate accounts of the state of the several branches of our Trade, formed upon long habits of experience, have been ever considered as of the highest authority. In the West India Trade, he has looked upon the late Mr. Ellis of Jamaica, and the late Mr. Walker, Agent for Barbadoes, as possessed of the best practical knowledge of it. These Gentlemen gave an interesting and exact detail in the year 1775, to the House of Commons, which was summed up in the most masterly manner by Mr. Glover. The testimonies of these Gentlemen have been supported by Mr. Edwards, whose equally good practical information and judicious sentiments on the subject, given by him to the World in a Pamphlet lately published, fully confirms those of the Author of these Considerations.

THE account of the Exportation of Sugar from the West Indies to America, which the noble Lord states to be very erroneous, was taken from Mr. Walker, whose information has been generally admitted to be very correct. In this instance, however, he appears to

have

have exceeded the real export, owing probably, to his either confidering the whole confumption of brown fugar in America as being the produce of our Weft India Iflands, or including the refined fugar fent there from England. But there certainly was a great part of the fugar imported into that Country of French, and other Foreign production. The account, there-fore, as it has been ftated, may be too much. But the real quantity cannot be obtained; nor indeed is it of any great confequence. The Tables given by the noble Lord, ftate that of Foreign at about 4,000, and the Britifh at about 7,500 hogfheads, at 1000 pounds neat weight to each hogfhead; which is, on an average, of each hogfhead, not fufficient. Mr. Edwards, who has taken great trouble in attempting to difcover the quantity, gives it at ftill lefs; but at the fame time he mentions the impoffibility of getting proper informa-tion from the Cuftom-houfe. The difference in opinion, of perfons otherwife well informed in the Trade, between our Weft India Iflands and North America, has been very great.

About

About 8,000 hogſheads ſeems neareſt the truth.
After all, if we can carry on our Weſt India
Trade with America, by bartering the Commodities of thoſe States for our produce, inſtead of
paying in ſpecie, it is immaterial what the exact
quantity is; for it muſt be merely ſpeculative.

In the accounts of the Fiſheries, the Produce
and Navigation of America, the Fiſhery of
Newfoundland, and the State of Canada and
Nova-Scotia, the Author has had ample and
exact details, from thoſe practically concerned
in them for a long courſe of years. He has alſo
availed himſelf of the knowledge of Mr. Wat-
ſon, the preſent Member for London, who laid
a very well formed and accurate account of
the American Fiſhery in 1764, before the Houſe
of Commons; from which time, to the commencement of the War, it wonderfully increaſed. To theſe authorities may be added,
a perſonal experience of above twenty years,
during which time, the Author has had many
and various accounts of the ſtate of the American Trade; and by which means he has

been

been able to combine the feveral materials of which they were compofed. Thefe he arranged during the laft Summer, with a view of throwing every poffible light upon a fubject of fuch importance to the Commercial Interefts and Naval Power of this kingdom; and which was then foon expected to become the object of Parliamentary Inquiry and Deliberation,

The Author having thus given his own authorities, will next take the liberty to fay a few words upon thofe of the noble Lord. They will be confined to his public authorities. His private ones, upon whofe information many parts of his Obfervations are founded, are of various kinds. In fome, great knowledge is difplayed, but fo much involved in hauteur and felf-fufficiency, that they defeat their own purpofe. But for others, all that can be faid is, that the noble Lord (he has too much good fenfe, information, and humanity, to have formed fuch opinions from himfelf), deferves great compaffion for having fallen into the hands of the perfons who have thus deceived him.

The

THE public authorities appear chiefly to be accounts of the Custom-house of Boston, all which the Author must consider to be of little or no authority. If the noble Lord desires a reason for his refusing to give credit to them, he will first say, that independently of its establishment, in opposition to the sense of that whole Continent, along with his own knowledge of the general practice in all Custom-houses, respecting those goods which do not pay duty, he has only to quote the noble Lord's own words, page 116 of the Observations, where he says, " It may " be here observed, that no very accurate idea " can be formed of the imports of America, " where the article was liable to high duties; " affording a temptation to the smuggler. " The extent of most of the ports, or rivers " leading to ports, affording almost an unin- " terrupted opportunity, where the inhabitants " were universally opposed to British Laws " and Regulations." And in page 44, speaking of a clandestine trade he says, " Through the " relaxed state of the Executive Powers of the " British Government in America, and the un-

" popularity

" popularity of the Revenue Laws, they found
" little difficulty or rifque in introducing (dif-
" ferent kinds of goods) through the various
" harbours, creeks, and inlets, with which the
" Northern Coaft of that Continent abounds."
Again, page 223, he fays " it is unneceffary to
" remark, that the value of the Imports and Ex-
" ports which was calculated from the Cuftom-
" houfe Accounts, is not perfectly exact, owing
" to well-known caufes;" to all which the
authority of Mr. Edwards, fpeaking of the
Cuftom-houfe in another part of our Colonies
(in page 19 of his Thoughts, &c.) may be
added : " The Cuftom-houfe Books (he fays) in
" the Weft Indies, out of which thofe docu-
" ments are formed, afford no certainty of
" information ; for many of the bays, creeks,
" and fhipping places in the Iflands, (parti-
" cularly in Jamaica) being remote from the
" ports of entry, it was formerly ufual with
" the Mafters of American veffels, loading at
" fuch places, in order to prevent delay, to
" make out their manifefts, and take out their
" clearances, before they were fully laden ;
                                    " receiving

" receiving afterwards on board, notwithstand-
" ing the risque incurred by the practice,
" much greater quantities of goods than they
" had reported. Governor Lyttleton, in a
" Reprefentation to the Lords of Trade in
" 1764, now before me, obferves, that there
" was not at any time, one half of the produce
" entered for exportation in the Cuftom-houfe
" Books at Jamaica, which was actually fhip-
" ped."

THESE opinions of the Cuftom-houfe at Bofton, will probably be thought a fufficient reafon for not confidering that Cuftom-houfe of
authority. Thofe which have a reference to
the Cuftom-houfes in the Weft Indies, muft
have the fame effect, particularly when they
relate to the exportation of fugar, upon which
the noble Lord has laid great ftrefs. They
will be partially fo with refpect to the
Cuftom-houfes in England.

IN all cafes of goods paying duty, the Cuftom-houfe accounts in England are very correct.

rect. The quantity of any goods paying duty, or any debenture goods, may be always exactly ascertained from their books. But these cases apply in very few instances to the Observations of the noble Lord; although he considers the Custom-house, in every point of view, and in all cases as affording the most authentic information. The fact is, except in particular cases, Custom-house accounts ought to be made use of for no other purpose, than for debenture goods, for goods paying duty, and for the comparison of our Trade at different periods.

THE Officers in the Custom-house, who have the charge of receiving entries of goods outwards, are as careful as it is possible for them to be; but the entry being obliged to be made previously to the shipping, the Merchants are seldom able to ascertain the quantity of goods which they want to ship. And when these pay no duty, they consider it to be no injury to Government, if they are not exact; provided they take care to give a regular account of the packages which are shipped, and on which the

fees

fees are to be paid. The copying the entry of ships in the Books is not always correctly done, nor sufficient care taken to distinguish British from British Plantation, and sometimes Foreign ships; by which means, though there is a clear distinction in the Register, this is frequently wanting in the account given of them. The Custom-house also, though they take down the name of vessels as they report, yet, from the circumstances attending their manner of entry, the number of ships cannot be, severally, ascertained; by which means neither their number or tonnage, are correctly known. The noble Lord indeed has made a remark at the latter end of his Observations, viz. " The " tonnage given in to the Register is upon an " average about a-third less than the real mea- " furement, in order to evade duties and ex- " pences, such as lights, &c.; but this is " more than counterbalanced by the tonnage " being in many instances repeated two or " three times; or as often as the vessel sails " from port in the same year." But surely his natural good sense must convince him, on re- collection, of the impropriety of calling such a

b   vague

vague calculation an authentic document by which our shipping may be ascertained ; especially as he does not himself always adhere to it, on the contrary, stating it to differ from the real tonnage one-half, one-third, and one-fifth, in the several accounts which he gives.

HAVING said thus much, some proofs of the Inaccuracy of the American Custom-house Tables may be expected. The accounts which he gives of the Imports and Exports to and from the two great ports of Philadelphia and New-York, are the most material, and shall be selected for the purpose. In the Tables No. 10 and 13 of the Second Edition, entitled, A General Account of Merchandize landed in the Ports of Philadelphia and New-York for two years, with the number of vessels employed, their tonnage, &c. the average tonnage of each vessel is rated in the first at no more than 41 tons, in the last at 60 tons burthen. In page 140 of the noble Lord's Observations, he mentions the number of ships belonging to Philadelphia, and partly owned in England and Ireland, never to have exceeded 280 sail at

any

any period. In page 28, he ſtates 1,150 ſhips
to have ſailed in 1775 from that port ; and his
Tables for the year 1773 make the number but
796, which, at an average of the tonnage, is about
60 tons, as has been mentioned. The noble
Writer makes the regiſtered tonnage of theſe 280
ſhips 15,000 tons, or 53 tons each upon an
average. If 1-fifth is added, as he gives it
in one place (upon American Cuſtom-houſe
authority) as the proper addition to make it
real tonnage, they will be 65 tons each; if
one-third part is added, as he makes it in another place, they will be 71 tons; and if one
half is added, which he in this place allows,
they will be about 79 tons on an average.—
The noble Lord muſt excuſe a remark in this
place, upon the variety of his calculations, and
how much they tend to miſlead. He was
obliged to increaſe his former calculations to
make a tolerable average. But if he had
doubled the tonnage which he had given, the
average of the Philadelphia ſhips would not
have been equal (ſuppoſing even the number
to be right) to the real burthen.

Upon

UPON this fubject of the built and tonnage of American veffels, the Author is induced to fay a few words more. It is relative to the Table of veffels and their tonnage, which the noble Lord has given in page 48 of the laft Edition of his Obfervations, as the account of the number and tonnage of veffels built in the feveral Provinces under-mentioned, during the year 1769, dated from the Cuftom-houfe of Bofton, and figned by the Infpector General of Imports and Exports of North America, and Regifter of Shipping; together with a Direction in the Account to add one-fifth part to the regiftered tonnage, in order to make it real tonnage. The Author has added the average of the tonnage of each veffel faid to be built in the feveral Governments, and fhall leave the confideration of the probability of this account to thofe perfons who are converfant in their trade, and the fize of their fhips.

Account *of the* Custom-House *at* Boston.

Provinces.	Veſſels built there, of all kinds.	Tonnage.	Average tonnage of each veſſel, and 1-fifth added.	
Newfoundland	1	30	36	If the Average of the ſhips built there each year for Foreign Trade is taken, (beſides ſmall veſſels) it will not be leſs than twelve, and thoſe in general large ſized veſſels.
Canada -	2	60	36	*Theſe are the two Colonies that are to make up the deficiency of American ſhipping.*
Nova-Scotia -	3	110	44	
New Hampſhire	45	2,452	65	The Author is not able to give an exact account of the veſſels built in theſe States; but he will venture to aſſert, and which he will at a future time prove, that it is very ſhort of one half the tonnage built in that year. In the Tables, No. 9. in the Second Edition of the Obſervations, the noble Lord himſelf gives 5,430 tons of new veſſels built *in Philadelphia only* in one year, from the 5th o. April! 1765 to the 5th of April 1766.
Maſſachuſetts	137	8,013	70	
Rhode Iſland	39	1,428	43	
Connecticut -	50	1,542	36	
New-York -	19	955	60	
Jerſeys -	4	83	25	
Pennſylvania -	22	1,469	79	
Maryland -	20	1,344	80	
Virginia - -	27	1,269	56	
North Carolina	12	607	60	
South Carolina	12	789	78	
Georgia - -	2	50	30	

Th

THE Author will not trefpafs upon the Public, in recounting the many inaccuracies in the General Tables of the Imports and Exports from the feveral parts of America, for the year 1770. To thofe who have leifure, he recommends an examination of thofe Tables, by comparing them with the quotations which the noble Lord makes, in the body of his Work, of feveral of the articles contained in them. It might be fuppofed, from the manner in which he has mentioned thefe authorities, that he would have paid a deference to them, by confining his references to the Tables; yet the accounts which he has inferted in the body of his Work, are chiefly thofe of the year 1769. He has indeed given fome articles of the year 1770; but they differ in fuch a manner from the Tables, that they do not appear to relate to the fame period. The following are inftances, viz.

In page 69 of the Obfervations.		In the General Table Exported.	
	Barrels.		Barrels.
Exported in 1770 pitch	15,793	Exported in 1770 pitch	9,144
tar	87,561	tar	81,422
turpentine	41,709	turpentine	17,014

Moft of the other articles in the Tables as materially differ.

THE

THE Tables of the Imports and Exports of this country, from 1770 to 1780, independently of the general inaccuracy, for the reasons which have been adduced, are not correctly given, considering them as comparative only. They cannot be a proper state of the American Trade, since they take in six years of the war; when the regular supplies were stopped, and those goods that were admitted, were carried clandestinely into the country, from the places in our possession. Nor have the General Accounts any agreement with Mr. Chalmers, (whom the noble Lord quotes) who has, in his Estimate of the Comparative Strength of Britain, given similar Tables; and who appears to have taken great pains to collect information. The value of the Exports to Africa, North America, and the West Indies, as estimated by Mr. Burke and Mr. Glover, in the account of the former, amounts to 6,024,000l. in that of the latter, to 5,900,000l. which is in effect the same. Lord Sheffield makes the amount of all the Exports to these places to be under 4,000,000l., a difference of no less than 2,000,000l. per annum. The noble Lord ap-

pears

pears to be equally inaccurate in his affertion, that our Foreign Trade has increafed within this century in an equal proportion to our Colonial. According to the accounts of the great authorities which have been produced, the Colonial Trade has increafed to twelve times its firft value, within that period; that is, from about 500,000l. to about 6,000,000l. a year; being nearly equal to the whole Export Trade of England at the time of its commencement; whilft, according to the fame authorities, our Foreign Trade has not increafed more than one-half of its then value. The Public will decide upon the difference of fuch opinions, and the weight of their authorities.

THE Author finds himfelf very difagreeably fituated, in being thus reduced to the neceffity of making remarks with fuch freedom, upon the Obfervations of the noble Lord; efpecially as feveral parts of them are replete with ufeful information, and appear to have been the refult of much labour, and a confiderable knowledge of many branches of our trade. It would give him
                                                                    much

much concern, if he fhould find that any ex-
preffions which he has ufed, are conftrued
into a want of that perfonal refpect which
he is very defirous of paying to the noble
Lord. He fhould have been much more
fatisfied to have waited patiently for the judge-
ment of that Public, to which both the
Obfervations of the noble Lord, and the
Confiderations of the Author, were fubmitted.
They were both written upon a fubject of great
importance; and the principles of each open to
inveftigation. But the Author having been, in
the Preface to the laft Edition of Lord Sheffield's work, feverely attacked, and affertions
(certainly through inattention in the noble Lord)
alledged to be made by him, which are not to
be found in his Work; he conceives himfelf
called upon, firft to juftify himfelf from this
particular miftaken charge; and next to make
ufe of every proper means to difcufs opinions
of fuch great and momentous concern to the
future welfare of the Public.

HE has made very few remarks upon the
particular parts of the American produce, or

of

of fome kinds of our manufactures, which Lord Sheffield has treated upon, and in which he has been greatly mifinformed; fearing that it would fwell this Work to too great a fize. It is already larger than he wifhed. He therefore referves himfelf for a further difcuffion of thefe. fubjects.

THE Author will now conclude in a few words. He has taken great pains to procure information of our Colonial Trade during a period of twenty years; both by correfpondence, and frequent converfation with many perfons deeply and extenfively concerned in it. The various accounts which he has thus perfonally collected, he has carefully compared with the beft authorities in this country, and has found no difference upon any material points. Having therefore the fatisfaction to find them thus generally confirmed, he cannot have a doubt, but that the feveral accounts, as they are given with fidelity, will be found as correct, as the nature of the fubject will poffibly admit.

CON-

CONTENTS.

PREFACE

CONSIDERATIONS.

State

Ruſſia

Opinion

The

A P P E N D I X.

E R R A T A.

W O R K.

———— 71, ———— 20, *For* the feare,   *read* thefe are.
———— 74, ———— 9, *For* two fifths,   *read* three fifths.
———— 87, ———— 13, *Dele* flax.
———— 88, ———— 1, *For* ot herwife,   *read* otherwife.
————113, ———— 16, *For* lumbers,   *read* lumber.
————114, ———— 9, *For* mentioned,   *read* mentions.
————171, ———— 9, *For* price,   *read* prices.
————172, ———— 9, *For* is,   *read* are.
————175, ———— 8, *Dele* comma.
————199, ———— 1, *For* fhip,   *read* fhips.

A P P E N D I X.

Claufe 11, Line 11, *For* or, *read* and.
Note to 12, Line 7, *For* independent, *read* independently.
Page 15, Infert 5s. drawback on bear fkins.
———— 19, *For* $\frac{6}{20}$ drawback on alum, *read* $\frac{16}{20}$.
———— 19, *For* $\frac{1}{20}$ drawback on alum Ronifh, *read* $\frac{12}{20}$.

CONSIDERATIONS, &c.

WHEN a man of rank, confideration, and of a character to which refpect is due, gives the fanction of his name to opinions in which matters of the greateft national importance are involved, his fituation in life, operating with the interefting nature of the fubject, can fcarcely fail to attract the public attention. But, if thefe opinions have been adopted without a proper confideration of the fubject; if, embracing great objects of Policy and Commerce, they are founded on falfe principles; if they tend to obftruct the happieft movements of

B

Govern-

Government, and to lead the Public into the adoption of fentiments and principles highly injurious to their interefts, the popular circumftances under which they were ufhered into the world, ferve, by giving authenticity to error and delufion, to render them more pernicious and dangerous.

In fuch circumftances, it becomes the duty of thofe who have had opportunities of knowledge and information on the fubject, and who are aware of all the mifchief and danger which would attend the adoption of fuch a fyftem, to endeavour to prevent the Public from being mifled by a fallacious reprefentation ; and, by an appeal to authentic documents, to fet them right in matters of fuch vaft importance to their commercial interefts. At the fame time that they deliver their fentiments with the freedom which the importance of the

fubject

subject requires, they should likewise do it with the respect that is due to the character of the Writer, and a deference to the motives which may be supposed to have influenced him : In their origin, perhaps, these might be good ; but, whether from a communication with designing or ill-informed men, or from whatever other cause, producing, in the event, effects miserably bad—In the hopes of making such a person feel a sense of the danger, the following advice of an elegant and philosophical Writer, in times very much resembling the present, may not be unseasonable :

—— *incedis per ignes*
Suppositos cineri doloso.

THE noble Author of the Observations upon the Commerce of the American States, did not weigh with the caution a

B 2   subject

subject of such magnitude required, the consequences of those principles which he has endeavoured so strongly to inculcate. He is desirous of convincing us, that this Nation, deprived of great and powerful Colonies in North America, can support itself by the means of its European Commerce, in a still more advantageous manner ; that the West India Islands may have the full benefit of their ancient supplies of lumber and provisions, either from this country, or our two remaining Colonies of Nova-Scotia and Canada ; and, in short, that we may now have a fuller enjoyment of Commerce, in a greater extent, and to a greater advantage, than in those times when the American States formed a part of our Empire.

Such are the principles which this Writer lays down, treating as " wild fal-
" lies of the imagination," every attempt

to

to procure the reftoration of our former commercial greatnefs, by the renewal of a clofe connection with America; the very means by which we attained it. He derives no fmall advantage, in the fupport of this erroneous doctrine, from the opportunity which the prefent ftate of things affords him, of playing upon the paffions of a people, fore with the lofs of a great and valuable part of their empire. But, if any faith is to be placed in experience, if there is any truth in the relation of the plain and fimple facts which will be given in the courfe of this Work, relative to the former trade between Great Britain and America, the reftoration of that trade, in as full and ample a manner as is confiftent with the fovereignty of each, is ftill fully practicable; and we have it happily yet in our power to make that country, formerly the child of our faireft hopes and expectations, our firmeft and

moft

moſt uſeful friend in future. If we have but patience to ſuffer their preſent paſſions to ſubſide, paſſions which the affecting events of the paſt few years muſt naturally excite in them, there is no reaſon to doubt of our obtaining every advantage which can ariſe from the ſtricteſt commercial union. However great their obligations are to France, manners, language, and ancient habits, will be too powerful opponents for that nation to overcome.

THE greateſt bar to the ſettlement of the American Trade upon a liberal foundation, is the natural propenſity of mankind to be governed by old habits. The attachment which we all have to the Act of Navigation, and upon which the noble Author ſupports his chief poſitions, is of this kind. For, having been accuſtomed to the proſperity ariſing from the flouriſhing ſtate of our Commerce, originally

nally fpringing from that Act, we caft our
eyes upon the whole mafs, without an
examination into its component parts;
or without a proper reflection upon the
effects to be expected from the late Revolution; and which the fhort time fince
the Peace, has not afforded fufficient practical opportunities to experience.

It is a quality applicable to the State as
well as to Private Individuals, that when
the objects of our purfuit are crowned
with fuccefs, we are never weary of
beholding their fruits. We look upon
them with pleafure and admiration. We
expand our views with their extenfion,
and folace ourfelves with the indulgence
they procure for us. But, if the continu-
ance of fuccefs generates felf-fufficiency,
pride, and diffipation, and that the fmiles of
profperity are turned into frowns, (the na-

B 4   tural

tural confequence of an alteration in our conduct) we are yet fond of refting on the fecurity of our enjoyments, and endeavour to
drive out the fenfe of prefent apprehenfion,
by the flattering hopes of a revival of our
former good fortune. Thus we ftumble on,
ftartling at every frefh diftrefs; till at
length, becoming familiarifed to calamity,
the impreffion ceafes, and with it all the
benefit of fuch frequent admonitions. Reduced to the ftate of a gamefter, ftaking
his all upon a fingle chance, we are divided between a hope of fuccefs, continually deluding us, and a falfe fhame,
preventing us from quitting a fituation
that is become burthenfome. We omit
the proper and the only means which remain in our power, the correction of our
errors, and the exertion of our beft endeavours, by courage, activity, and perfeverance, to regain our loft condition. Thefe
neglected, wafted by enormous expences

on the one hand, and cruſhed by heavy loſſes on the other, we ſink into poverty and contempt ; under the aggravating circumſtances, of their being produced by our own miſconduct, and our diſtreſſes rendered more poignant by the recollection of our former wealth and greatneſs.

THE mere ſound of words, when they relate to any intereſting object, has an aſtoniſhing effect in catching our attention, and affecting our paſſions. When this illuſion once faſtens upon us, it ſpreads like wild fire, ſubduing for a ſeaſon every obſtacle that is oppoſed to its progreſs. In this manner we are influenced by the Act of Navigation ; and in the warmth of defending the letter of that law, we entirely loſe ſight of the ſpirit of its conſtitution. The very name ſeems to convey ideas of reverence, if not of ſuperſtition ; and the Act is itſelf conſidered as an inexpugnable tower

of

of defence, furrounded and fortified with every ftrength that can be derived from old habits, and from former experience of its advantages. Sanctified by the opinions of the beft Writers upon Trade at the time of its being paffed, it has been delivered down from father to fon, as a fundamental law, which it would be a crime to difcufs, and in which, to attempt the leaft alteration, be the circumftances of variation in our Commerce what they may, would be little lefs than impiety. It is given to us as a law of the Medes and Perfians, " which altereth not."

But, though we cannot fubfcribe to the opinion of its being an inviolable law, we profefs a high veneration for it. We acknowledge its title to the proud and juft diftinction of the Maritima Charta, the Great Charter of our Commerce. It was the means of eftablifhing our Colonies.—

Thefe

These Colonies were the means of establishing our immense Navigation. Of the necessity and of the excellence of this *half-divine* law, as Mr. Glover, one of the ablest of our Commercial Writers, stiles it, the smallest doubt cannot be entertained, by any person who has seriously considered the subject. We are bound to admire the wisdom of its composition, as we are bound to admire the wisdom of the composition of Magna Charta ; the one being of as general importance to our Navigation, as the other is to our Constitution. Yet the various revolutions in our national interests have made it useful, necessary, and prudent, to make alterations in the great law of our Constitution. And the late revolution in our commercial interests has made it equally useful, necessary, and prudent, to make alterations in the great law of our Navigation.

THERE

THERE would have been no neceffity of bringing this Act to the queftion, had not the late revolution in America taken place ; for we had, by the means of our Colonies, attained to fuch a fuperiority of Naviga-tion, and in confequence, to fo great a command of the Carrying Trade in all parts of the world, that the Act itfelf became of lefs moment to the fupport of our Com-merce. From being a facred palladium on which the fafety of our Empire refted, it was at length become no more than a partial fecurity for the monopoly of our American Colonial Trade ; for, in many in-ftances, we were obliged, for our mutual advantage, to furrender it to them. And as our union with America is now dif-folved, if we do not fpeedily and earneftly endeavour to refume (as nearly as the pre-fent circumftances of the two countries will admit) our former fituation, the Act of Navigation will return to the fame ftate in

which

which it originally paſſed in the laſt century—*An Act ſimply for the preſervation
of our own ſhipping*—The loſs of our Colonies precluding all expectation of its re-
ſtoring our Carrying Trade.

At that time, the trade of the kingdom
was in the hands of a few opulent men;
but when our Colonies increaſed in
ſtrength, and the principles of Commerce
became better known, its extenſion exceeded imagination; and even ſurpaſſed
the wonderful Republic of the United Provinces, which had turned its dreary fens
into warehouſes, filled with the richeſt
merchandize of every quarter of the globe;
and from wanting food for its own ſubſiſt-
ence, had ſtored its granaries with food for
nations. With even ſuch rivals, the good-
neſs of our ſhips, the facility of working
them, the ſkill and activity of our ſeamen,
and the expedition with which they conveyed

veyed goods from market to market, gave them a preference in every port that they entered : Not only in the tranfportation of goods to Great Britain, which might be legally imported in foreign fhips, but alfo in the Carrying Trade of foreign nations. The natural means then to regain this preference, is to recur to thofe habits and maxims by which it was obtained.

THE prefent fupporters of the Navigation Act, in its legal fenfe, proceed upon the fame principles, with refpect to the American States, as the framers of that Act did with refpect to the Dutch. The quality of induftry is, however, the only circumftance common to thofe nations. Every other widely differs. The Dutch had been long our enemies; were our rivals both in Commerce and Manufacture; they lived at our doors; and participated to fuch a degree in every branch of our trade, that they

they carried away almoſt the whole profits. A vigorous meaſure was therefore neceſſary for our preſervation. The Navigation Act was paſſed, and much praiſe is due to the Authors of it; ſince, independently of its other great conſequences, it fully anſwered the moſt ſanguine expectations of the Merchants, and merited the commendations which Sir Joſiah Child, one of the great Traders of thoſe times, gives it. The Americans, on the contrary, cannot for ages be our rivals in Manufacture; they live at a diſtance that will always prevent an interference, contrary to our inclinations; they have been our fellow-ſubjects, and the great means of our being maſters of the Carrying Trade; their ſhipping forming, in the view of the ſhipping employed in the Commerce of theſe kingdoms and the Weſt Indies, about two parts in five; and of the ſhipping of Great Britain only, almoſt one-third. Should, therefore, the opinion of thoſe to whom alluſion

allufion has been made, who are now more
ftruck by the folemnity of the found, than
influenced by the efficiency of the fpirit of
that Act ; and who do not diftinguifh between a partial alteration for the admiffion
of American fhips, upon terms confiftent
with the principles upon which it was
made, and the total renunciation of thofe
principles;——fhould (it muft be repeated
and urged) fuch opinions prevail, we fhall
have no means left to us, with equal facility and cheapnefs, of fupplying their
places; and the remaining parts of our Navigation will require every fecurity, which
the ftrictnefs of the laws, and vigilance in
their execution, can afford them. For, as
we fhall be driven within the limits of our
own fhipping, by adhereing to the letter
of the Act of Navigation; and as there
will then be other nations, who will be
able, in their fhips, to carry on even our
own trade to the greater advantage of our

Mer-

Merchants; this pledge of the forecaft of our anceftors will be no lefs than the Citadel itfelf, to which we muft retire, after enduring the mortification of beholding the admirable and extenfive out-works forced out of our poffeffion.

THE noble Author of the Obfervations declares the Carrying Trade to be the chief object to which he directs his views. To this laudable purfuit all our views muft be equally directed. But, though we fully agree upon the advantages to be derived from this Trade, we widely differ as to the means of fupporting it: And we cannot forbear comparing the endeavours of the noble Writer, in this inftance, to thofe of an impatient and confident operator, who hews off, without mercy, thofe wounded limbs which a temperate and fkilful application might reftore to their former ufe in the corporeal functions. The fymmetry of the perfon may fuftain injury, but the

C   ufeful-

ufefulnefs will remain. Our empire has fuffered by its Colonies having been fevered from it; but good fenfe and moderation will repair the breach, and retrieve the fplendour of its former condition.

To demonftrate, therefore, our inability to preferve the Carrying Trade, without the affiftance of America, better evidence cannot be produced than the account of the fhips employed in the Commerce of this Ifland, and the places where they were built, taken from the actual furvey which is made of them, from time to time. Of thefe, the number of fhips built in the American States formed almoft one third. If the account is extended to the Trade of the whole Empire, in which the Weft Indian connection with America makes a large additional part, the proportion will be about two parts in five. The account of the fhips employed in the Commerce of Great Britain, at the beginning of the

American

American war, and at this time, are as follows : The number of ſhips, or the tonnage, differ very little. At the former period there were about 1300,000 tons; at the latter nearly the ſame. The ſhips were built in the following countries :

	Ships.
Northern parts of Great Britain	2,419
Southern — —	1,311
Ireland — —	199
Britiſh Colonies ſtill remaining	163
American States —	2,342
	6,434
Foreign Countries —	1,260

being 7,694 ſhips employed in the Commerce of Great Britain at the commencement of the war. Soon after the peace the numbers were as follows, viz.

Built

	Ships.
Built in the Northern parts of Great Britain —	2,226
Southern —	1,088
Ireland —	144
Britifh Colonies ftill remaining	104
American —	1,126
	4,688
Foreign Countries —	2,892
	7,580

But as a proportion ought to be allowed of the foreign fhips for prizes, which will replace fuch of our veffels as were taken by the enemy, the accounts will nearly be,

Britifh —	5,154
Foreign —	2,426
	7,580

Or confidering the American fhips as foreign,

Britifh and its prefent dependencies	4,028
Foreign —	3,552
	7,580

THE

THE foregoing account proves, in the first place, that if at this time, American built ships are confidered as foreign, ships of that defcription are almoft equal in number to thofe Britifh built; forming feven parts in fifteen, or nearly one half of the fhipping employed in the Commerce of Great Britain, after proper allowance is made for the prizes taken by us, to fupply the places of thofe taken by the enemy. And next, that although for the want of fupply, the American fhips were reduced more than one half, yet that the deficiency was not fupplied by Britifh fhips, but by veffels foreign built, of which the Northern Nations fupplied the far greater number; and fo confiderable was the increafe of foreign bottoms, that even Flanders, Portugal, and the Italian States, whofe whole joint ftock before the war amounted to about a dozen fhips, fupplied almoft four hundred.

THIS

THIS view of the ftate of our fhipping, points out to us the neceffity of endeavouring to convince thofe of their errors, who are for cafting away our former Colonial Commerce with a marked difdain; left the eftablifhment of fuch prefumptuous opinions fhould be the means of its being loft to us, and with it every hope of our regaining the Carrying Trade. America was always able to fupply us with fhips thirty per cent. cheaper. than they could be built in Great Britain, even with the difadvantage of having the cordage, fails, and ftores, exported from hence.* Cargoes of goods were often fent out in barter for fhips; which, as well as fhips built for fale, making a freight home, the purchafe could be made on ftill cheaper terms by the Britifh Merchant. This advantage

---

* In New England, the fhip-builders will now contract for building fhips at 3 l. fterling per ton, including the joiner's work. In the River Thames the price is 9 l. per ton, for the carpenter's work only.

vantage in purchafe enabled our Merchants to trade upon a lefs capital; of
courfe fubject to lefs infurance and intereft of money. Not only all the purpofes
of our own Commerce, but thofe of the
Carrying Trade, were fully anfwered.—
They were alfo frequently purchafed in
England by foreign nations; a circumftance which feems to have efcaped the
notice of the noble Author, as he dwells
much upon the impoffibility of the Americans difpofing of their fhips to any other
nation than Great Britain; and, (which is
yet more aftonifhing, and muft be attributed to inattention, as in other parts of his
works he is of opinion, that our remaining Colonies fhould not be permitted to
build veffels exceeding fifty or fixty tons)
that fhip-building will increafe fo faft
in Canada and Nova Scotia as to leffen,
and ultimately to deftroy that bufinefs in
the United States. The hazarding fuch
affertions is very mifchievous to thofe

C 4   who

who are not converfant with thefe Colonies; as it holds out a very fallacious
idea of their fituation, and exhibits an
imaginary profpect, which can never be
realifed : To men of knowledge and information of the State of Canada and Nova
Scotia, they carry fo much improbability
with them on the firft view, that they
fufficiently refute themfelves.

THE prefent queftion is, how to fupply the deficiency which the want of
American fhipping will create, without
lofs ? The mere deficiency may be fupplied : We may purchafe foreign fhips,
though on bad terms. But the dearnefs
of Britifh built fhips (the price having
increafed from five and fix pounds to nine
pounds per ton, for the carpenter's work,
within a few years, and a certainty of its
being ftill higher, if there fhould be an
additional demand) will, if we are confined

fined to them, effectually deprive us of
the Carrying Trade, and greatly enhance
the prices of building our ships of war.

It may be objected, that although British
ships are dearer, they are better, and will
laſt much longer. Merchants of great capital, and regular trade, do not regard this
additional expence; for in general they con-
trive to hold as ſmall a ſhare in the ſhipping
as they can, dividing the property amongſt
their tradeſmen, who make themſelves
amends by being employed in the repairs.
The inhabitants of the Northern Ports of
Great Britain, are the only people who
make Britiſh built ſhips a profit; and
this is owing to their frugality both in
building and ſailing their veſſels. The
general purpoſes of Commerce are directed very differently in our times, from what
they were in former days, when the whole
was in the hands of a few rich men, and
accordingly

accordingly produced immenfe profits.
The capitals of our Merchants at prefent
are no ways proportioned to the trade
which is carried on. But credit fupplies
the place of capital, and the profit, by being more diffufed, becoming lefs to the
individual, it is neceffary to reduce, as low
as the feveral branches of our Trade will
admit, the amount of the money employed
in them.—The lefs that is, the lefs will the
intereft and infurance be upon it; and the
gain or lofs be proportionate. The very
faving of intereft and infurance, in the
courfe of a few years, will much more
than compenfate for the difference in good-
nefs of the veffels. The following inftance will illuftrate this affertion.

	£.	s.	d.
* A Britifh fhip of 100 tons, will coft to fea — —	1,300	0	0
Carry over £.	1,300	0	0

* 13l. per ton, is a very moderate calculation, applicable only to the cheapeft building ports. A River built
fhip would coft much more.

| | £. | s. | d. |
| Brought forward - | 1,300 | 0 | 0 |

Intereſt of money per
   annum   -   £.65 0 0

Inſurance about ſix
   pounds per cent. per
   annum   -   78 0 0

               £.143 0 0

Which, together with intereſt upon
   it for ten years, will amount to   1,799   15   0

                    £.3,099   15   0

Suppoſing the ſhip, at the end of
   that time, to ſell for   -   599   15   0

There will remain   —   £.2,500 0 0

A Britiſh plantation ſhip of 100
   tons, purchaſed in England, will
   coſt to ſea   —   800 0 0

Intereſt of money per
   annum   -   £.40 0 0

Inſurance at the ſame
   rate as the Britiſh
   ſhip   - —   48 0 0

          Carry over   £.88 0 0   £.800 0 0

	£.	s.	d.	£.	s.	d.
Brought forward	88	0	0	800	0	0
Which, together with interest upon it for ten years, will amount to				1,105	11	0
				£.1,905	11	0
Supposing the ship, at the end of that time, to fell for only	-			105	11	0
There will remain			£.1,800	0	0	

As the freights will be equal in both vessels, which the charge of fitting out on the different voyages is supposed also to be, the calculation is made upon the first cost, the interest of money, the insurance, and the addition of interest upon these charges, which is always included in mercantile transactions. The difference, therefore, of expence, between a British and an American built vessel, will not, in the

course

course of ten years, be less than 700l. *
upon so small a capital. If there is any
error in this calculation, it is in favour of
the British ship: For, if an account is
kept of each vessel, supposing the same
certain freight made, and the same certain outset paid by each, and interest of
money, and insurance is calculated, the
American ship will clear herself in six
years; whilst the British ship will not ac-
complish it in less than ten, and much
longer, if a River-built ship; (the value of
each being considered at the several periods as stated above;) which will leave a
still more considerable balance than the
above 700l. in favour of the American
ship. Every man versed in mercantile affairs will see the truth of these observations.

SOME

---

* This difference in a River built ship, would be several
hundred pounds more.

SOME objections may be made, by thofe who have had the misfortune to meet with a New England fhip, badly built, againft the fuppofed equal charge of fitting out. The Merchants, in general, find very little difference, particularly in fhips of the Middle and Southern States, whenever they fall into the fhip carpenter's hands. But to guard againft fuch cafual inftances, the calculations are not only made for the firft ten years, when fhips (except in cafes of accident) are liable to few other than common repairs; but the Britifh veffel is fuppofed to be capable of fervice, and is valued at nearly half the original coft, whilft the American fhip is confidered as not fit to be fent longer to fea, and is valued at no more than fhe will fell for to break up.

To carry this comparifon yet farther—The American fhipping employed in the
Commerce

Commerce of Great Britain (exclusive of
the trade between America and the West-
Indies) at the commencement of the American war, was 398,000 tons, which, at
the moderate calculation of 13l. per ton,
will cost   —   £.5,174,000
8l. per ton   —   3,184,000

Making a difference of   £.1,990,000

Additional capital employed in our shipping, or above 218,000l. per annum, for
interest of money and insurance charged
upon our trade.

THE American built ships, which have
been given in the account of the shipping
employed in the Commerce of Great
Britain, must not be confounded with
those ships which carried on the trade between this country and America. The
former

former were incorporated in the general
body of our fhipping, of which the American trade was only a part, and which
was carried on by the American Merchants in fhips, whether of the built of
Great Britain, America, or any other
country, indifferently, as they came into
poffeffion of them, or chartered them for
the voyage. The account, therefore, of
the American built fhips in our trade, the
burthen of which was 398,000 tons, muft
be confidered as applicable only to the purpofe of fhewing the ftate of our fhipping,
from whence we drew our fupplies, and
how the deficiency is to be filled up,
fhould the American built veffels in future
be excluded.

It will be ufeful to us, to take into our
confideration the ftate of the fhipping
employed in the Commerce of America
before the war. There not being the
fame

fame regularity in furveying the trading veffels of that country, as is practifed in Great Britain, and the Cuftom-houfe books not diftinguifhing the voyages which each fhip made in the year, it is not poffible to give fo very exact an account. But good information, collected with care, and compared with the produce of the different States, to which equal attention has been paid to procure the beft accounts, very fully fupplies the deficiency; fufficiently, at leaft, to give us a very juft idea of the ftate of their fhipping. Before the war, the number of veffels, of all defcriptions, employed in tranfporting the produce of the American States to Europe, the Weft Indies, and other parts of America (exclufive of thofe employed in coafting the Creeks and Rivers of each State, of which no account is neceffary to be given, as they had no connection with any foreign trade) amounted to above 4,400,

and

and were of the burthen of upwards of 400,000 tons. They were thus divided:

	Ships.	Tons.
In the European Trade were employed about	1,220	195,000
In the West India and Coasting Trade -	2,150	146,000
In the New England Fishery, besides those employed in carrying the produce to market, which are included in the above -	1,099	59,775
	4,469	400,775

Of these, the shipping employed in the West India and Coasting Trade, and in the Fisheries, were almost wholly American property, and manned by American seamen; as on the contrary, those in the European

European trade (which were about one half of the shipping employed in the Commerce of the American States) were generally the property of British Merchants, navigated by British seamen, and carrying to the markets of Great Britain, directly or circuitously (the latter in a small proportion only) the produce of those States.

THE danger of losing our seamen, particularly in time of war, has been the cause of very serious apprehension; the same common language creating a difficulty of distinguishing the American from the British seamen. The principal means of averting this evil, which menaces us in a most alarming manner, is to endeavour, on our part, to unite our common concerns upon such grounds, as to make it the interest of America to enter into an agreement, for the purpose of establishing such a description of the seamen of each country,

D 2

as

as will prove their identity. This might
be always practically done, in those vessels
which are the joint property of the subjects
of both nations, and to which a certain
number of British seamen must always belong, by rating the names, country, and description of every seaman on board, both
British and American; to which reference
might always be had. Besides, the more
the mutual interests of both countries are
blended, the more exertion will be made by
the States to prevent the desertion of our
seamen, as their own safety will then be,
in a great measure, involved in it. On the
contrary, if America is considered merely
in the light of a foreign nation, and treated
with as such, she will have no motive of
friendship or attachment to induce her to
put a stop to a measure, which, though
an evil of magnitude to us, will prove of
essential service to her, and consequently
be her interest to encourage.

THOSE

THOSE who point out the inconveniences which the United States will probably feel, from a want of connexion with this country, do not sufficiently advert to the circumstance of our being at the same time, and for the same reasons, partakers in their sufferings. Nor are the complaints which they make of America's engrossing the Carrying Trade (" which, considering our situation and circumstances, "they say, we had comparatively little " of;" and in consequence are of opinion, that even at the price of the enormous expence of the last war, the separation is of advantage to us) to be reconciled to the insignificant light in which they at other times view the American Navigation and Commerce; removing by the one all fear of rivalship, and overthrowing by the other the great superiority of our Navigation. The real fact is, the more America increased in her Commerce and Na-

vigation

vigation, the greater was the acceſſion of ſtrength to this country, and the greater in proportion was the increaſe of our own ſhipping.

Any attempt to prove, that America, by having obtained Independence, will feel inconvenience in the loſs of the Carrying Trade, muſt be nugatory, and founded on miſinformation; the ſuperiority of ſhipping being on the part of Great Britain. The United States, in general, are much more in want of veſſels to carry off their produce, than of being carriers for others. Foreign nations will ſupply their preſent wants, if we refuſe; and neceſſity, ſupported by their own natural advantages, will make proviſion for their future ones. But it is very bad policy to decline the preſent benefits which are held out to us, and to ſtimulate them to be rivals to our Navigation, when proper encouragement

(which

(which the experience of former advantages ftrongly points out to us) would, by poffeffing the better capital, throw the direction of their Commerce chiefly into our hands, and be the means of renewing our former friendly intercourfe. It cannot be too often repeated, that the nearer we approach to our former commercial connexions, the nearer approach we fhall make to the intereft of this country.

WE fhould be faithlefs ftewards indeed, of the talents which have been intrufted to our care, fhould we reject a Commerce in every refpect beneficial to us; fupporting our Carrying Trade, by employing a great number of veffels, particularly in the tranfport of the bulky articles of the Middle and Southern States; and forming no lefs than a fixth part of our whole fhipping, equal, if not fuperiour to that of our Weft India Colonies. Thefe States, deriving fo much

D 4 greater

greater benefit from husbandry, have no
inclination to carry it on for themfelves;
nor will ever be induced, either to employ their own exertions, or make ufe of
the fhipping of our European neighbours
for the purpofe, if we will undertake it in
a manner fatisfactory to them. This we
may do, with equal fatisfaction and advantage to ourfelves.

This advantage is not, at leaft in many
points, denied by the noble Writer; but
he builds his opinion wholly upon the
idea of America's having infulted Great
Britain by the declaration of Independence;
and therefore confiders any permiffion
whatever, for the United States to trade
with this country, to be a favour, which
we are very indulgent to grant, and which
they ought to receive with gratitude.—
However confident he may be of this pofition, he certainly does not act with
policy,

policy, to accompany the terms of trade which he thinks proper to be offered to thofe States, with an avowed declaration of thefe fentiments; fince he cannot forget the difpofitions which they fhewed during the feverity of the war, and that, by a parity of reafoning, although the terms held out might have advantages, yet if they were couched in the language of dictation, they would moft probably be rejected. It is at all times a moft difficult part for a nation, which has mifcarried in the attempt to fubdue by force fubjects who have refifted, and maintained an independence of her Government, to convince them that fhe has loft all views of again endeavouring to reduce them. Pride and arrogance will, if there is fufficient power to make them feared, excite refentment; contempt, if there is not. There is no other method to recover their loft affections, than a Treaty, clearly founded

on

on a broad bafis of mutual advantage.——
It is in this cafe a fortunate circumftance,
that the general interefts of both countries
have fo intimate a connexion, that any
contrary fyftem muft be productive of confiderable prefent inconveniences to that
which adopts it. And, ultimately, of
much greater detriment to Great Britain
than to the American States.

THE noble Writer has made it a queftion
for our confideration, " Whether we have
" not engaged too great a proportion of
" our capital in foreign trade, to the
" great detriment of other important na-
" tional concerns, and particularly of the
" moft important of all, Agriculture,
" which at this moment languifhes in a
" great degree, by the fcarcity of money.
" It would be found (he fays) on inveftiga-
" tion, that not half of the money is em-
" ployed in it that fhould be, and that in many
                              " parts,

" parts, the farms are by no means pro-
" perly ftocked and cultivated. It is alfo
" well known, that the price of land has
" fallen near one-third within eight or
" nine years." The firft idea which naturally ftrikes us on reading thefe words,
is, that the Writer of them is an entire
ftranger to the tranfactions of the laft
twenty years; to the profperous ftate of
the firft ten years of that period; to the
gradual decay of the laft. The flourifhing
condition of our Agriculture and Navigation, before the unhappy difputes with our
Colonies; the large fums laid out in the
improvement of land; its high and increafed value; the immenfe tracts of
wafte grounds enclofed and fertilifed, and
the general opulence of our farmers; together with the great extenfion of our
Commerce and Manufactures, and the
abundant wealth of our Merchants and
Traders before that period; when compared

pared with the miferable contrast fince
that time, point out very clearly the caufe
of thofe melancholy effects which have
been thus defcribed. A part of the one
hundred millions of money fpent in thefe
difputes, might have been applied to thofe
purpofes, which the noble Author of the
Obfervations laments, are neglected for the
want of affiftance.

THERE is one, and one argument alone,
which can be urged, with any appearance
of reafon, in favour of that fyftem which
confines our fhipping within the bounds
of our own country. It is founded in defpair; and fuppofes that the National Debt
is become fo enormous, the taxes upon
trade fo great, and a relaxation of fpirit
fo general, that our own fhipping will be
abundantly more than fufficient for all the
purpofes of our Commerce. If thefe melancholy furmifes prove to be facts, the
game

game which we are playing, to preferve the Carrying Trade, is at an end; and we fhall find fufficient difficulty to keep even the immediate Navigation of Great Britain and Ireland in a tolerable condition. Whatever opinion may be formed of the bad fituation the country is in, the man who recommended acting upon fuch defperate principles, would find himfelf feverely condemned, even by thofe very people who conceived that opinion. They would very properly tell him, that exertions ought at leaft to be made, to recover, as far as we were able, the loffes we have fuftained. A very confiderable part of our dominions has been torn from us. But though its fovereignty is gone, we ought not to fit quietly down, under an infatuated blindnefs, and be witneffes of its Commerce following, when it is in our own power to retain it; and by that means put ourfelves in a condition to recover our former

mer

mer commercial, and in confequence, our
national greatnefs. Let us not lie down,
like men in defpair; but be active, refo-
lute, and work out our falvation with fpirit and perfeverance.

It will be proper to take a view of the
former Colonial Commerce of this country, and the authorities upon which the
accounts are given, in order to form a
judgment of its value. The firft account
is taken from an original Manufcript of
Davenant, quoted by Mr. Burke; and is
merely to fhew the rapid increafe of our
Plantation Trade. The latter accounts, the
greater part within our own experience,
and fully proving the magnitude of our
North American exports, are taken from
the comprehenfive and enlightened fpeech
of Mr. Glover, in fumming up the evidence of Mr. Ellis, and Mr. Walker, before the Houfe of Commons, upon the

Bill

Bill for Reſtraining the American Trade. Such an authority will not ſurely admit of diſpute.

At the beginning of this century, the Exports to North America and the Weſt Indies, were - - £.483,265

Africa - - 86,665

———————

£.569,930

The Exports were, on a medium, from 1739 to 1756,

North America only - £.1,000,000
Weſt Indies - - 700,000
Africa - - - 180,000

From 1756 to 1773,

North America - £.2,300,000
Weſt Indies - 1,100,000
Africa - - 470,000

On

On a medium of the years 1771, 1772,
1773,

North America	-	£.3,500,000
West Indies	-	£.1,300,000
Africa	- -	700,000

And proportioning such a part of the African Trade as belonged to North America, the Exports will be found to be, at a medium of the three years before the war,

North America	-	£.3,650,000
West Indies	- -	1,850,000
		—————
		£.5,500,000
From Scotland	- -	400,000
		—————
		£.5,900,000

Or in proportion of two thirds to North America, and one third to the West Indies. The whole being upwards of one third part of the Exports of this kingdom, estimating their value upon the same accurate authority, at sixteen millions, during the few years preceding the American war.

THE

THE proportion of Britiſh goods to foreign goods, exported from hence to North America and the Weſt Indies, were to the former, three fourths Britiſh and one fourth foreign; to the latter, two thirds Britiſh and one third foreign. The exports of Britiſh Manufactures will then be in this proportion:

North America —	£.2,737,000
Weſt Indies -	1,234,000

THE accounts which were taken by authority in America, of the value of Britiſh goods, imported previous to the war, are ſomewhat, though not materially, different. They were eſtimated as follows:

To the four New England

States - -	£.407,000
New York - -	531,000

E   Carry over £.938,000

Brought forward	£.938,000
Pennſylvania -	650,000
Virginia and Maryland	865,000
North Carolina -	25,000
South Carolina -	365,000
Georgia - -	50,000
Jerſey and Delaware no eſtimate, ſuppoſe -	50,000
Sterling	£.2,943,000

THESE accounts, marking as they proceed, the aſtoniſhing increaſe of our North
American Export Trade, which had its
riſe almoſt within this century ; and
which, within ſo ſhort a ſpace, attained to
the immenſe ſum of three millions and a
half ſterling, do not, great as they are,
confine our ideas within even ſuch ex-
tenſive bounds. For, ſhould ſuch a
perfect reconciliation between the two
countries

countries take place, as to produce the
revival of our former connexions, we
may look forward to a yet greater increafe of our Navigation and Commerce,
in the increafe of American population;
which, according to the beft Authors,
doubles itfelf in twenty five years: And
as the inhabitants have fo great an extent
of fine country, to employ them in the
more eligible cares of Agriculture, their confumption of Britifh Manufactures would
neceffarily be of wonderful magnitude.

Such an increafe of trade, of courfe
demanded an increafe of fhipping. We
found it in thofe States, which the fupporters of the contracted fyftem of Navigation are ftriving to tear from us. They
feem weary of the profperity of their own
country, and are ready to abandon the
only opportunity which prefents itfelf to
us of reviving our own Navigation, by
fuch a communication with America, as

would prevent foreign nations from the benefit of supplying the present want of shipping, which the war has occasioned in that country. But instead of a conciliatory healing conduct, they are goading the United States into the use of those powerful natural means, which the situation of their country has given them ; and which will enable them, in a course of years, as they increase in strength, not only to deprive us, but every other nation, of the Carrying Trade.

They have excellent harbours, and they build ships cheaper than any other people. The improvements they make in that art are exceedingly rapid. If we choose to procure them from these ports, once so familiar to us, by a free admission of them as British ships, upon stipulated terms, in the manner of ships taken as prize, or when they are the joint property of the inhabitants of

both

both countries, it is in our power to do it. America has fhewn us the example : The State of Maryland having paffed an act upon the ceffation of hoftilities, declaring all Britifh fhips of which the Citizens of their State held one third part only, to be deemed fhips of the State, and to be entitled to the privileges of fuch fhips. We fhall then fecure our fupply of fhipping, as well as the fupport of our manufactures of cordage, fail-cloth, and many other ftores, neceffary for the fitting out fhips, which they will otherwife buy of the Northern Powers, or manufacture for themfelves. They have as good hemp as any in the world, and naval ftores in great plenty ; fail-cloth they can import, of equal quality, and upon cheaper terms, than from this country. Of their induftry and perfeverance we have had the moft convincing proofs. We experienced the good effects of their commercial fpirit

E 3

before

before the war ; we were witneffes to thefe
qualities in them, under all the feverity of
that calamity.   We beheld their fhips of
war, and almoft their whole trade, nearly
annihilated at various times ; yet, they
were continually building more, which
were as fucceffively taken from them ; and
there were not wanting variety of inftances, where veffels being taken, were
repeatedly replaced by the owners with
others, to an incredible number.   In one
inftance, not lefs than thirteen times.—
And as a further proof of their fpirit in adventure, feveral fhips fince the Peace, have
been fitted out for China, and Difcoveries
in the South Seas.   Nor was the appearance of Philadelphia, foon after the evacua-
tion of it by Sir Henry Clinton, lefs aftonifhing. At that time, one miferable ferry
boat, and the remains of a few half burnt
gallies, were all the objects that prefented
themfelves to the view, upon the folitary

waters

waters of this once flourishing place.
A gloomy spectacle of desolation filled
the eye. In a very short space of time,
the sound of the axes, and the noise of
the shipwrights, re-echoed through the
port; and within twelve months, a fo-
rest of ships covered the rolling waves of
the majestic Delaware.

Examples like these, ought to teach us the
wisdom of securing a people, who are so
capable of being made useful friends, or active enemies. It would be prudent to bid
even high for such industrious consumers
of our manufactures ; and to form such a
connexion, as will make America, instead
of a dangerous rival to our Navigation,
conducive to the common interests of both
countries ; more particularly as those
branches of our Carrying Trade, which
are not within the limits of the Act of
Navigation, and are of great importance

to

to us, will certainly be loft, without the
incorporation of American, or other
fhipping equally cheap. And even thofe
which that Act fecures, cannot be carried
on with equal advantage, becaufe the
more our Navigation is confined, the
greater will be the charges upon it, whilft
its late general extenfion was productive
of as general benefits, diffufed through
every part of our Commerce.

A GREAT ftrefs is laid upon the neceffity
which the Americans will be under to purchafe Englifh goods, from their not being
able to procure them in any other country
upon fuch cheap and advantageous terms.
It is, however, a hazardous attempt to
drive them to this neceffity. Mankind are
formed of materials which have a great
aptitude to refift, when force is employed.
They may be led, but cannot eafily be
driven; and though, according to the
noble

noble Author, a Stamp Act, a Tea Act,
or any other fimilar Act, cannot again
occur, yet the exclufion of American fhips
from our Weft India Iflands, has already
produced fome meafures injurious to the
admiffion of Britifh fhips, and the importation of Britifh goods. One of the States
has already laid a conditional duty of
about three fhillings per ton on the former, and of two per cent. additional on
the latter. The prohibition of the import
of Oil, has not yet reached New England. By the laft accounts from
America, the Merchants had determined
upon a general revifal of their Trade,
and increafed powers were to be given to
the Congrefs, for its regulation in the feveral States. The Americans have been
in the practice of felf denial already. A
patched, thread-bare coat, was thought
no difgrace during the war. Nor
were the firft women in the country
aſhamed

aſhamed of being employed in making linen for the uſe of the common Soldiers. We cannot ſuppoſe, that the miſeries which America experienced from the ravages of the war, though ſmothered over at the peace, are entirely buried in oblivion. That can alone be effected by good will. Irritation may make the wound bleed a-freſh. We ſhould act wiſer to attempt a radical cure.

We certainly manufacture many ſpecies of goods cheaper and better, and from the ſuperiority of our capitals, and ſkill in Commerce, can afford to ſell them on more advantageous terms, than any other nation. Theſe are coarſe woollens* of every kind, worſted ſtuffs, iron ware, nails, cutlery, common earthen ware, glaſs,

* The Merchants of Philadelphia have lately imported ſome coarſe woollens from Hamburgh, which proved ſatisfactory to them, both in quality and price.

glafs, tobacco pipes, worfted and cotton
ftockings, fhoes, buttons, hats; all kinds of
Manchefter and Norwich goods, gauze, filk
ribbons, fewing filk, tin plates, fheet lead,
and all forts of lead and plumbers' work;
pewter, copper, and brafs ware; painters'
colours, cordage, fhip chandlery, uphol-
ftery, and cabinet ware; fadlery, gunpowder, books, ftationary, beer, and
porter. There may be fome articles
omitted in this enumeration.

THE Americans already manufacture cordage, fail-cloth, hats, ftockings, glafs, and
porter. But they are in a forced ftate, and
will not be brought to a perfection yielding
profit, if they have a free and fatisfactory
trade with this country, as they will be
able to import cheaper than they can manufacture. To reafon as the Author of
the Obfervations does, upon America's
not having any coal, clay, flint, or fimilar
materials, for manufacture, and to recom-
mend

mend " the shutting up of the collieries
" of Cape Breton, in order to encourage
" our own coals, and the Carrying
" Trade," hardly merits a serious answer.
It is the first time that coal was supposed
to afford profit to ships carrying it such
a voyage. Let us not deceive ourselves
by such ideas. America is 1300 miles
in extent along the coast. In depth im-
mensely great, and it contains all that is
to be found in Europe. She has lead,
iron, and copper mines ; and if we will
trade with her satisfactorily, she will send
the raw materials for us to manufacture.
She has coal in abundance, clays of all
kinds ; even the finest porcelain clay,
equal to the Chinese ; and in these heavy,
cheap articles (except casually for bal-
last) she cannot be supplied from distant
countries ; but when she is in want of
them, she must provide herself at home.

Upon

Upon many of thofe enumerated goods we already grant confiderable bounties, to encourage their exportation. Thefe will, in courfe, be continued. They are,

On gunpowder   4s. 6d. per 100 pounds

On linen $\frac{1}{2}$ to $1\frac{1}{2}$d. per yard

On fail-cloth   2d. per ell

On filk   6d. to 4s. per pound, according to the different qualities.

On refined fugar   26s. per 112 pounds

On cordage   2s. $4\frac{3}{4}$d. per 112 pounds, if exported to Europe, and it fhould likewife be extended to America.

Of thefe manufactures, filk will be preferved partially. The leffer parts manufactured at Coventry, and the mixture of it with cotton and worfted at Manchefter and Norwich, have fo much greater neatnefs and fancy than thofe of other countries,

tries, that they will certainly command a preference. The other parts of the filk manufacture have too many difadvantages to contend with, to expect any other fale than what may arife from being part of afforted cargoes of goods. The greater expence of raw materials and wages in England, muft fecure, in every cafe, this trade to France.

THE great bounty on refined fugar feems to give it a preference at almoft any market. The Americans, however, appear to be very jealous of its introduction, and have laid extraordinary duties upon it in fome States. For gunpowder and cordage we may expect a demand; but the manufacture of fail-cloth is in danger of being loft to us, the quality of that commodity being excellent, and to be procured on cheap terms, in other countries.

WE

WE have one chance of preferving the Linen Trade, by the foftnefs of texture of the Irifh linen. The threads are more unequal, and therefore more pliable than the German ; a quality which is generally preferred in linen.

IF the Americans continue to be fupplied with goods from this country, there does not appear to be any abfolute neceffity for taking away the remaining duties on foreign goods exported: But no more muft be exacted than on goods exported to other foreign countries. It would without doubt be an encouragement; but the revenue is in fuch an impaired ftate, that if it incurs this reduction, fome other addition muft be made to it. The demands of the Merchants in America, will not for a confiderable time be equal to the fale of whole cargoes of any one fpecies of goods ; and the port charges attending veffels lading

in

in different places, will exceed the favings made by purchafing the foreign goods they want in any part of Germany or the Baltic, of which they are the growth or manufacture. It will often happen, that a fhip is ordered to return home with fuch a quantity as may be wanted from any of the above ports to which they have brought a cargo. But this will be accidental, and is not connected with the afforted cargoes of goods, which the Americans will give orders for to this country. Foreign goods generally form a fourth part of an afforted cargo.

THERE are many articles which America will fupply herfelf with, by the return of her veffels from the Southern parts of Europe, without coming to England; fuch as filk, wine, oil, and other productions of thofe countries. The climate of the

the Southern States is fo perfectly well
adapted to the culture of thefe articles,
that in time they will fupply themfelves.
They have no other difficulty to contend with, than what arifes from the
infancy of thofe parts of the country.
They want only manage ment, and fufficient population, to furnifh themfelves
with every product of the fineft countries of Europe and the Eaft. They
will be in pofleffion of thefe advantages,
long before they turn their views to manufacture. We fhall always find a protection to ours in the greater profit, health,
and enjoyment, which attend hufbandry ;
efpecially in a country where the fineft
land may be had, almoft for the culture.
The inhabitants of fuch countries will
prefer purchafing, to the manufacturing of
goods for their own ufe. Neceffity has
fometimes driven them to it. Cotton and

flax

flax they have; and fo long fince as the war of 1739, the Carolinians, on the mifcarriage of their European fupplies, manufactured cloathing for their Negroes. In the back countries they yet manufacture for their immediate ufe: Very much in the fame manner as was formerly practifed in this kingdom, (probably, in the interiour parts of Wales and Scotland the cuftom may ftill continue; if not, it is in the remembrance of many perfons of our times) where all the apparel and linen, neceffary for the family, were made in it. They fowed the feed, raifed the flax, dreffed it, and prepared both that and the wool for manufacture, which was performed within their own domain. Their wants were not many, and thefe were fupplied among themfelves. But as it happened in England, it will happen in this part of America; the country will

be

be better peopled, the roads will be more opened, and they will find it more profitable to purchafe goods, than to manufacture them.

THE exportation of goods from America comes next under confideration, and how far it may be made ufeful to us. The United States of North America may be divided into three parts, each having a particular connexion with the different States of which it is compofed. The firft in order is New-England, whofe trade chiefly confifts in fhips built for fale, in exporting lumber and provifions; but more particularly in the fifheries, which they have purfued with great fuccefs. The fecond divifion is from the River Hudfon to the Chefapeak, including the States of New-York, the Jerfeys, Pennfylvania, Delaware, Maryland, and Virginia; all con-

F 2

nected

nected together by a trade fimilar to each other; principally in wheat, flour, tobacco, building fhips, lumber, and provifions. The laft divifion is North Carolina, South Carolina, and Georgia; the former of which produces wheat, lumber, and naval ftores; the latter, rice, indigo, lumber, naval ftores, and provifions.—— This is the outline of the Commerce of America. To fpeak more particularly, we muft begin with New-England, whofe great Commerce is the fifheries of cod, whale, mackrel, &c. from which are produced fpermaceti, whale, and cod oil, and whale bone; together with fhips built for fale, pot-afhes, fome naval ftores, fkins, furs, mafts, boards, joifts, planks, ftaves, cattle, horfes, hogs, poultry, beef, pork, hams, butter, cheefe, &c. alfo fome manufactured iron ware, hats, and candles. The exportation from the Hudfon-River,

River, and the Bays of Delaware and Chefapeak, confifts of tobacco, wheat, flour,
bread, Indian-corn, beans, peafe, rye,
beef, pork, tallow, hogs-fat, wax, flax-feed,
fome naval ftores of various forts, afhes,
horfes, drugs, hams, fmoked beef, butter,
cheefe, live hogs, poultry, hemp, flax, deer-
fkins, brandy, iron-ore, bar and pig iron,
copper, furs, fhips for fale, and lumber.
From the Carolinas and Georgia, they export rice, indigo, deer and other fkins,
hemp, hides and other tanned leather;
lumber, pitch, tar, turpentine, fome tobacco, Indian-corn, wheat, flour, horfes,
and live ftock, beef, pork, butter, hogs-
fat, wax, tallow, drugs, hams, and fome
fhips. They have attempted filk and
wine, with an appearance of future fuccefs. Oranges are fine, and in plenty.—
The feare the exports of the United States,
and the divifions in which they are na-

F 3   turally

turally placed. The amount of the value of each, previous to the war, were nearly as follows, together with that of the tonnage employed in the exportation :

First Division.

Tons of shipping employed.

New-England States, (including the fisheries) £.770,000*   150,000

Second Division.

New-York,   £.529,000
Philadelphia,   685,000
Maryland,   379,000
Virginia,   706,000   £.   Tons.
              —————— 2,299,000   183,500

              Carry over £.3,069,000   183,500   150,000

Third

* This exceeds most of the accounts generally given; but those were taken many years ago, and did not include the very great increase of the fishery in the few years preceding the war.

Tons of shipping employed.

Brought forward £.3,069,000 183,500 150,000

hird Divison.

forth Carolina,£.78,000
outh Carolina
 and Georgia, 532,000
—————— 610,000 66,500
—————————250,000

Sterling, £.3,679,000 employing 400,000
tons of shipping.

THOSE which have been part of the importations into Great Britain, shall first be
mentioned, and next those sent to the
West Indies.

ONE of the most material branches is
ships built for sale, at prices greatly inferiour to those in the cheapest ports of

F 4   this

this kingdom. The carpenter's prices for building, in sterling money, by the ton, were as follows : In New-England three pounds. In the Middle States about four pounds. In South Carolina, of live oak, five guineas ; the whole cost of the ships equipped for sea, seven to ten guineas. They were chiefly from New England, which supplied about ~~two~~ *three*-fifths of the whole number of the American ships employed in Great Britain, and were generally sent to sea at the expence of about *six to* seven ~~to eight~~ guineas per ton. The most beautiful are those built in Philadelphia, where this art has attained to the greatest perfection; equal, perhaps superiour, to any other part of the world. Capital ships have also been built at New-York, and in the Chesapeak; and in South-Carolina, of live oak, which is of much longer duration than any other timber whatever.

THOSE

THOSE who have afferted, that the fhipping of our out-ports, are equally lafting
with the American fhips built of live oak,
have been very much mifinformed; the
latter being found by experience, to be
much more durable than our beft oak.
Nor has the noble Writer been under a
lefs error, in placing fo much dependence
upon American Cuftom-houfe Accounts.
A more ftriking inftance of inaccuracy
cannot be given, than in the account he
gives, (from that Cuftom-houfe) of the
fhipping built in America in one year.
We muft naturally fuppofe, from this account, that Newfoundland was not a Colony where fhips were ufually built. Yet independently of fmall veffels, there is no
year in which many large fhips are not built
for foreign Trade. Generally twelve, upon
an average. The Obfervations on the
American Trade alfo vary much, in the
difference between real and regiftered
tonnage; in fome places one-fifth, in
others.

others, one-third, and in one place one half.

THE Fishery, and carrying the fish to market from New-England, employed at the commencement of the war, about 1450 vessels of 100,000 tons burthen, and 11,000 fishermen and seamen. This account not agreeing with that of the Author of the Observations, requires some explanation. He estimates the shipping employed in the different fisheries in 1763, as follows: In the whale fishery eighty or ninety sloops; in the cod fishery two hundred and fifty schooners; and in the mackrel fishery forty sail. We had a very accurate account of these fisheries, from a Gentleman of the first commercial knowledge, and of long practical experience in the American Trade, Mr. Watson, Member for London, given by him to the House of Commons in the year 1775;

1775 ; taken nearly at the fame period as that of the noble Author; the latter being in 1763, and Mr. Watfon's in 1764. The difference between thefe accounts are very great. Mr. Watfon made the number of 'veffels employed in the whale fifhery to be one hundred and fifty, which the noble Author eftimates to be ninety. In the cod fifhery three hundred, which he makes to be two hundred and fifty, and in the mackrel fifhery ninety veffels, inftead of forty.

From the year 1764, to the commencement of the war, the Fifheries gradually increafed; at which time they were become aftonifhingly great. In the Cuftom-houfe accounts, which the noble Author has given of the exports of 1770, there is a confiderable difference from that which he has inferted, in the body of his Work, as the produce of 1772. But the fame
objections

objections operate at all times to Custom-house accounts, and in particular to American. He makes the whole produce of the cod fishery alone, to amount to eight hundred and fifty thousand quintals of dried, and forty two thousand barrels of pickled fish; of which three hundred and seventy thousand quintals, and forty thousand barrels, he states to be of the American fishery. This account, as well as that of Newfoundland, appears to be taken from the Custom-house, as they are much under the real state of those fisheries. But this being always the case with these accounts, the entries being under-rated to avoid payment of fees, or similar demands, one third part may at least be generally added to it, which will bring it near the truth.

THE American Fisheries were in this increased state at the commencement of the war, when the accounts given in this
Work,

Work, combining all parts of them, the
cod, whale, mackrel, and fhad, were taken.
They are very correct; and will be found
to agree with the beft information collected
at that period.

THE produce of the cod fifhery of New-
England is divided into two-fifths of falted
cod-fifh for the European market, remit-
tances for which were fent to Great Britain,
to pay for goods purchafed there; and
three-fifths for the Weft Indian mrket, to
which place the mackrel and fhad were
fent. The produce of the whale fifhery
is fpermaceti and whale oil, and whale
bone; which, as well as the greater part
of the cod oil, was fent to Great Britain,
and will yet center there, as it is the beft
market they can procure for it. Our confumption of oil is very great, and a part
of it, as well as whale bone, is neceffary
to our manufactures, and therefore to be
confidered as a raw material. The permiffion

miſſion, therefore, to import it, will be of ſervice to both countries. A different opinion ſeems lately to be entertained; the Proclamation iſſued out at Chriſtmas laſt, not permitting its importation. One conſequence will probably follow; that is, as much deficiency or delay in payment for the manufactures we have already exported to New-England, and an equal want of ſale of them in future, as we could barter for this commodity.

THERE has been always a difference in the duty charged upon theſe articles, according to the quality of the veſſels in which the fiſh were caught. Oil, and whale fins, taken in ſhips belonging to Great Britain, are imported duty free. If taken in ſhips belonging to the Plantations, oil pays thirteen ſhillings and two-pence one-fifth per ton, whale fins two pounds fifteen ſhillings per ton. If taken

in

in foreign shipping, the duty amounts to a prohibition. These duties, which are very moderate, may continue; or if it is supposed not to be a sufficient difference for the encouragement of our own fisheries, such greater duties may be imposed, as will serve to quicken their labours, yet not prevent the importation of American oil; or create any material additional expence to our Manufacturers, or to the consumption of commodities necessary to us.

An idea has been suggested, of suffering furs to be imported duty free, provided a free passage was granted to our Canadian subjects through the American States.——This is intended to remove any disadvantage which this country may derive from the boundary line cutting off the country of the Illinois from Canada. At present, the Hudson's Bay Company have so great a proportion of this trade, and the Americans,

ricans, by their fituation, poffeffing alfo a
great part, what remains will not be of
any great confequence. It will be of expence to the Revenue, as furs pay a duty
on importation. Beaver, on account of
our manufacture of hats, pays only 1d.
2-20th each fkin.

THE motive for this propofal is to encourage the fur trade in Canada. But it
would be alfo making the United States
powerful rivals in it. Befides, the good
effects of Colonization in North America
are now loft to us, and it will be much
more profitable to avail ourfelves of the advantages, which we may obtain by means
of our former Colonies, (who will increafe
in population fafter than we can increafe in
manufactures to fupply them) than be at any
great expence in improving our remaining
Plantations on that continent. It is im-
poffible to form any judgment of the future

ture inhabitants of the extensive internal country of North America; or whether there may not be many independent sovereignties. We have but one part to act. To keep on good terms, and to trade, if we can, with the whole country. Every other encouragement to Canada, than that which will produce an adequate immediate benefit, will be, in the present circumstances of North America, only forwarding a sovereign establishment there.

It is difficult to say, what may be the effect of taking away the bounty on naval stores. Some say, that the quality of American tar and pitch is not equal to those of the Baltic; that there is a heat in the former, which does not agree with the manufacture of cordage so well as the Baltic tar; which is also clearer, though the American is equally good for other purposes. This account may, however,

G   proceed

proceed from interefted perfons, in the hope of purchafing them on low terms; it having been frequently the practice with refpect to Carolina indigo, which was bought cheap as fuch, and then fold for French. The Legiflature, in order to give encouragement to the improvement of tar, granted a bounty of ten fhillings each barrel, under the denomination of green tar, defcribing the quality which it was neceffary to have. Whether it was owing to want of care, or the difficulty of making it, very little was fent from America entitled to this bounty. Common tar received a bounty, after deduct-ing the duty which was paid on impor-tation, of 4 s. 9 d. each barrel. Pitch, de-ducting the duty, in the fame manner, about 9d. the hundred weight; and the duty upon turpentine exceeding the bounty, there was actually paid about 8 d. the hundred weight; mafts and bow-fprits

were

were fubject to no duty, and received a
bounty of 20s. the ton ; all paid in Navy
Bills, which generally bear a heavy dif-
count. The price of tar in general was
from 7s. to 9s. the barrel ; fometimes it
was as low as 6s. whilft at the fame
market, Baltic tar fold from 11s. to 12s.
Pitch commonly brought 5s. the hundred ;
and turpentine was very variable in price.
The bounty (except turpentine, upon which
a duty was paid) generally paid the freight,
which was a great encouragement ; yet
naval ftores were always an unprofitable
remittance. By thefe bounties ceafing,
the Revenue will be benefited, but the
price paid by the confumers muft increafe,
and our fhipping and cordage may alfo
be affected by it. The duties, therefore,
at leaft, fhould be taken off. The prices
of the Baltic tar and pitch will rife in
proportion ; for wherever the demand is

G 2   increafed,

increafed, the price of courfe increafes with it.

If the fame duties are charged upon American naval ftores, as upon thofe of the Baltic, the former muft give up the trade,. as they will never be able to enter into competition with them. Their diftance, and the extraordinary expences they muft be at, forbid it. The fame reafon may be applied to mafts, which now receive a bounty of twenty fhillings the ton ; it is that bounty which can alone fupport them againft thofe of the Baltic ; where, by longer practice, they render them of much better quality.

The noble Author of the Obfervations is of opinion, that the Territory of Penob-fcot in New-England, fupplies the only good mafts in North America. But although the mafts there are excellent, and it ha

hitherto

hitherto produced the chief fupply, he is by far too confined in this affertion, that it is the only country where good mafts are to be procured; as they may be now had in many parts of the United States, and in time they will be more improved in the making them. The Cyprefs tree will afford moft excellent mafts. Moft probably he means, that Penobfcot is the only good place to procure them in that part of the country, referring particularly to Nova-Scotia.

THE duties upon hemp, flax, pig and bar iron, and afhes, may be placed upon the fame ground as thofe of the Baltic. If the charging them at lefs, creates any rifque of unpleafant difputes with Ruffia, there is no advantage to be obtained in this country by it, adequate to the confequence. The American hemp, though of an excellent ftaple, is not well cleaned, and therefore not fo proper for ufe as Ruffian.

It

It is ot herwife, in many refpects, fuperiour in quality; and when the fault of negligence in dreffing it is remedied, it will be equal in quality to the beft Ancona Hemp. It has one advantage even now; the maiden hemp, as it is called, not being taken out of it when exported. The Ruffians are in this practice, in order to preferve it for their own ufe. One principle, indeed, pleads ftrongly for hemp and iron not paying duty; which is, their being a raw material. For to tax raw materials, is to tax the manufactures which are produced by the labour of our own people. But, fo great is the difficulty of finding other ways and means, to fupply the place of thefe duties in our impaired revenue, that the very attempt terrifies us, and prevents our attention to thefe capital branches of our manu-factures. We fhould yet take care, that we are not preferving a fmaller, at the hazard of lofing a greater object. In their prefent ftate of importation, how-

ever,

ever, there is not sufficient reason for making any difference in the duty, unless it might prove the means of preventing the Americans from manufacturing their iron.

THE free importation of lumber and staves has been of service; for as the quality of what has been generally imported here (except white oak staves, which are very good) is inferiour to that of the North of Europe, they are purchased on lower terms for cheaper purposes, and will not in fact bear a duty. The Americans have wood fit for all purposes. The Cedar and Cyprefs in particular, are very fine. They will probably come into very general use amongft themfelves. But we have not given any encouragement for their importation.

DEER fkins are of great use to our manufactures, and do not fuffer by the duty

G 4   which

which they are charged with. No alteration is neceſſary in the articles of chocolate, ſpermaceti candles, or other ſimilar articles, where an interference with our own manufactures occaſioned high duties to be impoſed.

MAHOGANY, walnut, lignum vitæ, or any wood uſed in the cabinet, joiners, or block-makers trades, though not of the produce of the United States, yet their conveyance through that channel having hitherto proved uſeful, their importation from America ought of courſe to be ſtill continued upon the ſame terms as formerly.

To Dye woods, every attention ſhould be paid for facilitating their importation, as they are of the greateſt conſequence to our manufactures. Theſe are, Logwood, Fuſtick, Nicaragua wood, Braziletto,

ziletto, and other kinds of materials for the dyers ufe. Indigo comes under this clafs; but in order to encourage the making this country an entrepot for American commodities, the duty on export fhould be taken off. Logwood is now in a more precarious ftate of being procured than ever. And Fuftick, by the lofs of Tobago, where great quantities of fine wood were cut, will be more fcarce.

WHEAT and flour, will of courfe be fubject to our corn laws, the importation depending on the neceffity we may have for them.

FLAX feed is an article of importance to Ireland, the want of which, fubjects that country to great difficulty.

THE articles of Commerce exported from America, have been generally, and thofe

thofe which relate to this country, particularly mentioned, except the two great objects of tobacco and rice. Thefe, from the proportionate fmall confumption. in this country to the growth, have the principal reference to the policy of making Great Britain an entrepot for them, as well as any other commodities, which, though of lefs confequence, come under that defcription. The adopting of this principle is neceffary for the prefervation of this part of the American Trade, and it will probably do more : It will make] Great Britain the centre of American Commerce in Europe. France has taken the lead : She has declared four of her ports, Free Ports, for the reception of American goods. If we act as wifely, we need not defpair of prevailing over her. But our Cuftom-houfe fyftem is now fo clogged, that it operates almoft as a prohibition. The port charges upon their

fhips

ſhips are very conſiderable, being charged
as foreigners, and ſubject to the payment
of double lights, though their caſes are
in many reſpects different, even conſidering
America as a foreign nation. For, the
payment of double lights by foreign ſhips,
was owing to the Dutch formerly doubling
that charge; in which they were followed
by the Powers in the Baltic; and the example thus given, was copied by us as a
matter in courſe. The Americans feel
this charge the more, as they were formerly not ſubject to it; and as they have
few charges of this kind in their own
country.

AMONG the different American commodities for which this country may be made
an entrepot, tobacco is the moſt capital
article; and the relation of the circumſtances attending it, will ſerve for other
goods in ſimilar caſes. A Proclamation
has

has indeed been lately iffued, which gives liberty to the Merchants to land tobacco without a depofit ; but as the former inconveniencies were not perhaps fufficiently known, and as even the repetition of an affair of this confequence is pardonable, if it will enforce the reafons for carrying this Proclamation into permanency, the former method may not be improperly introduced at this time.——— When tobacco was landed in England, a depofit was required of 4l. per hogf-head, to be drawn back when it was exported. In London, the warehoufes allotted for its reception by the Cuftom-houfe, lie at a great diftance from the quays; and upon thefe it is not fuffered to remain, though landed on one day and to be fhipped the next, even with a watch upon it. The expence of landing, cranage, wharfage, porterage, cartage, warehoufe-rent, and a numerous train of

. Cuftom-

Cuftom-houfe and other charges (upon the whole of which, though the duty was to be received back, the Merchant charged his commiffion) amounting to a large fum, was, with the duty, generally drawn upon the foreign port to which the tobacco was to be fent, which made a very large advance of money. In three or four months the Merchant received back the duty he depofited, which, after deducting the charges, he remitted to the perfon abroad. Thus, a medium cargo of tobacco was charged with an advance of about 2000l., almoft its firft coft, for feveral months ; a great part of which was funk in unneceffary charges, commiffion, intereft of money, and lofs by re-exchange.

THE remedy for thefe inconveniencies is found to be very eafy. Upon the arrival of any cargoes of tobacco, rice, or any goods not ufually, or only partially, confumed

confumed in this country, they fhould be fuffered to be landed, under bond, free of duty, and put into a warehoufe under the locks of the Officers of the Cuftom-houfe, and the locks of the Merchants, generally called the King's Warehoufe, in the fame manner as is practifed in the importation of coffee and rums. This method is fafe, and without difficulty. The duty is paid when the goods are taken out for home confumption, or the bonds difcharged when exported. This will make our ports (fo far as refpects an entrepot for goods imported from America) in a manner free ports. The fmall expence incurred upon their goods, and the expeditious difpatch of their veffels, advantages always to be met with in free ports, are great temptations to Merchants. Indulgencies as fimilar as the nature of our Cuftom-houfe will admit, fhould be granted.

To

To guard againſt the objections which may be made by the Cuſtom-houſe, to the admiſſion of American goods, duty free, for export, (as an encouragement to them to make this country an entrepot) ſome remarks upon the preſent conſtruction of our Trade Laws are neceſſary. Formerly, the ſpirit of thoſe Laws was the governing principle of the Officers of the Cuſtoms. Lately, they have too great an aptitude to be governed by the Letter. The Exciſe, having no other object in view than the mere collection of internal duties, has a plain, confined ſyſtem to follow, from which there can be little or no deviation. The Cuſtom-houſe, on the contrary, having the whole Commerce of the Empire under its management, and the Trade Laws not being ſufficiently explicit (from the impoſſibility of conforming them to the variety of circumſtances which attend our foreign trade) their application

muſt

muſt be left to the wiſdom of thoſe who
preſide over it, and whoſe conſtruction of
thoſe laws ought always to be of the moſt
liberal kind. For ſome years paſt, this has
not been ſufficiently attended to. The deſign is to prevent ſmuggling, but unfor-
tunately it is conceived, that the more trade
in general is confined, the better the object will be attained. The conſequence
is, that the Merchants are loaded with
new regulations, increaſing the difficulties
of the honeſt trader, already ſuffering from
the inroads made upon his trade by the
ſmuggler: And whilſt the defrauder of the
Revenue, notwithſtanding all the precautions that are taken, imports vaſt quantities
of goods without entries, the moſt diligent
watch is kept over thoſe at the Cuſtom-
houſe, in the common mode of buſineſs;
and goods paying no duty, run the riſque
of confiſcation, if there is the ſmalleſt miſ-
take made in the entry. Men of eſta-
bliſhed character in trade, and there are

none who bear a higher reputation for probity than the Britiſh Merchants, ought not to be thus lumped in one general maſs of ſuſpected perſons. It implies, that all traders are objects of ſuſpicion.— This is bad policy. If a man is honeſt, it will have a tendency to weaken his attempts to diſcover any practice to the injury of the Revenue ; and if he is inclined to roguery, he will turn ſmuggler himſelf.

ANOTHER remedy is wanted to be applied in the Cuſtoms, which relates more particularly to the trader, and would afford very great ſatisfaction to him ; would be the means of ſaving much time and trouble, and render the preſent complex and almoſt incomprehenſible practice of the Cuſtoms ſimple, and eaſy to be underſtood. If ſuch a correction was carried into execution, it is probable that the Revenue would be benefited by it. At preſent, the various branches of the Cuſtoms

being

being obliged to be calculated, with their
difcounts, in all entries of goods, they require a great deal of time, and are only
known to the Clerks of the Cuftom-houfe.
The Merchant is not fufficiently acquainted
with them, and takes them very unfatif-
factorily upon truft. The firft ftep in fetting about the correction of this grievance,
fhould be, to direct the Cuftom-houfe to
draw out an account of all goods which pay
duty, imported into, and exported from the
kingdom, for a certain term of years before
the war, in order to form the average of
the actual confumption. A communication
with men of bufinefs, in the different trades
of which each article is a part, will ftill be
the means of further knowledge. When
thefe accounts are obtained, and a knowledge of the actual confumption procured,
with the circumftances attending each
fpecies of goods, they fhould be valued according to their prices, and the duty added
to, or taken from them, as the neceffity of
the

the cafe required. The value of goods, since they were firſt rated, has very conſiderably altered. Some goods are charged with too heavy a duty in proportion to their value; others do not pay enough. By this means the duties in general will be more equally proportioned to the goods upon which they are charged. The duties on goods ſhould alſo be a ſingle ſpecific charge, without fraction, and the whole of the duties be reduced to a fund, conſiſting of one branch only. Some advantage to the Revenue will be made by the fractions. At the ſame time, the ſyſtem of drawbacks ſhould undergo a reviſion, in order to afford as much encouragement as poſſible to make this country an entrepot. To carry this correction into ſtill more advantageous execution, the high duties, which the Merchant is now obliged to pay before his goods are landed, and which occaſions a conſiderable additional capital to the coſt, ſhould be

H 2   paid

paid to the Excife; and fo far as relates to the connexion with the Cuftoms in the entry, might be tranfacted in the fame manner as coffee, rum, and fuch articles. The former prejudices againft the Excife, muft be removed by the ftrict and fevere execution of the Laws of the Cuftoms. It gives no alarm to the honeft trader; the roguifh one makes the noife. All high duties are beft collected by the Excife; becaufe they are then not paid by the Merchant till his goods are fold to the Confumer, and he is by that means eafed of the burthen of making a large and unneceffary advance of money. Such, or fome other effectual means, are indif-penfibly requifite to be put in practice, or the Revenue will ftill fuffer further de-creafe, and our Commerce be more and more impaired.

With thefe very fimple regulations, England might be made an entrepot for American com-

commodities. The principal articles are to-bacco and rice: About one hundred thousand hogsheads of the former have been annually imported into this kingdom, of which about twelve or thirteen thousand have been left for confumption in Great Britain; the reft was exported to different parts of Europe. About fixty thoufand barrels of rice were formerly imported; the chief part of which was afterwards fent to Holland and Germany, the confumption in England being very fmall. Seventy thoufand tons of fhipping, almoft wholly belonging to Great Britain, were then employed in bringing thefe articles alone to market in this country. The fame trade, the fame employment for fhipping, and owned by Britifh Merchants, may yet be continued to us. Even the fupply of France we have a very great chance of poffeffing;

the

the Farmers General having already be-
gun to make confiderable purchafes in this
country.

It is poffible that the Portuguefe may
import rice as formerly. Their attempt
to introduce Brazil, inftead of Carolina
rice, which the noble Author has dwelt
much upon, is not the firft which they
have made without fuccefs. Whatever
may be the event, their prohibition of
Carolina rice can be of no advantage to us.
Perhaps the contrary; as any deficiency
in the fale of Carolina rice, may prove, from
the want of fufficient means, an equal
deficiency in the fale of Britifh manufactures. It was from neceffity that the Portuguefe procured any other fort. The
Dutch have done the fame ; but both prefer Carolina rice. The inftance given by
the noble Author, of a fhip arrived at Lif-
bon from South Carolina, which would
have

have come to a better market in England, proves nothing, becaufe the price both here and in Holland happened then to be enormoufly high. The returns in goods, hould the Portuguefe admit rice, will be chiefly in wine. But this exportation of ice directly from South Carolina, to the Southward of Cape Finifterre, was permitted by Act of Parliament, and is one of hofe inftances in which the Act of Navigation was obliged to be relaxed. The difappointment of a private individual, was he caufe of rice being made an enumerated article, to be brought to Great Britain only. He was a Merchant of great influence in this country, and annually fent hips to Carolina, at a time, when the export of that commodity was very trifling. A Colonift having built a veffel, tranf-ported in it part of the produce, deftined or them, before their arrival. This difappointment proved the immediate occafion

H 4   of

of rice being enumerated, which continued, till the prohibition became manifeſtly
injurious ; and then permiſſion was granted
to export it to the Southward of Cape
Finiſterre, as formerly ; firſt, in Britiſh
ſhips only, and afterwards extended more
generally. A valuable trade muſt otherwiſe have been loſt to this country.

THE Germans and Dutch will continue
their purchaſes in Great Britain. For
England may be conſidered as a great Inn,
on the road from America to the Northern
parts of Europe, where the Americans
may repoſe themſelves, till they procure
knowledge of the beſt market to ſend
their goods. Formerly, rice was landed,
ſhifted, and put in order for a market, in
the Southern ports of this kingdom, chiefly at Cowes, paying a duty of 8d. the
hundred weight. Tobacco was ſuffered to
remain in the ſhips that brought it, which

were

were confidered as warehoufes, in order to
avoid the payment of the duties, until
the Merchant had a demand for fale; when
he landed the quantity he wanted, paying
duty for one part, and giving bond for
the remainder, which he took out of the
fhip; the firft for home confumption, the
other for exportation; and when the laft
was again fhipped, and the debenture paffed
in the common forms, the bonds which
had been given, were of courfe difcharged.
As fhips were formerly confidered as warehoufes, the fcene is only to be changed to
warehoufes on fhore, and the prefent method, in every other refpect, and which is a
very fimple one, continued in ufe.

It will be proper to take into confideration, the ftate of Canada and Nova-Scotia,
previous to that of the Weft India trade;
for we have been given the ftrongeft affurances, in the Obfervations to which reference

rence has been so often made, of the sufficiency of those two Colonies to supply all
the lumber, live cattle, and provisions,
which our West India Islands formerly received from the American States. If we
will trust to Nature, she has declared very
strongly against these assertions, by shutting up their ports six months in the year;
and what must particularly strike our attention, which has been directed to the
advantages that the West India Islands are
to receive from thence, is, that the hurricane
months occupy the greater part of the time in
which the Navigation is open. Independently of this severe tax, it is further to be observed, that neither the Canadians, No-
va-Scotians, or any other people situated
at 3000 miles distance from the seat of
their Government, (even ours, excellent as
that might be made, not excepted) have the
same powers of applying their natural advantages, as those immediately under a Government

ernment of their own. How much worfe then muft be their fituation (as in the prefent cafe) when an induftrious rival neighbour, with fo many fuperiour advantages, lives at their very doors. This fuperiority is not to be overcome, until the country which attempts it has a good Government, becomes equally well peopled, and has fufficient capitals to carry on their trade. It is of little confequence to fay, there is lumber enough in Canada for all our purpofes, and that it may be rendered of ufe; whilft that Colony has not, what all Colonies muft have to make them ufeful, a fufficient number of people to cut down that lumber, and a good Navigation to carry it off. We cannot doubt the Southern parts of Canada being a good country; but the advantages are all internal, and can never be made ufe of for the purpofes of Commerce, till the country on the Ohio, and in the Illinois, is fettled. And when that is

done,

one, who is to reap the benefit of it? Not this country, for the paſſage cannot be by the River St. Lawrence.

THE length of the winter in the ſettled part of Canada, deſtroys all the effects which the labour of the ſummer produces; ſo far as reſpects the carrying on any conſiderable Commerce. During the war, the quiet ſhe enjoyed threw the Indian trade into her hands, which the ſuperiour advantages of the American States will now deprive her of. Canada has produced undoubtedly a great quantity of wheat. But the Americans were the chief purchaſers of it. When grain was ſcarce in Europe, before the late war, an unuſual demand was made upon America, and the Merchants of Philadelphia, who were great ſpeculators in that article, ſent Agents to Canada for the purchaſe of corn, which they diſpatched ſhips for, and conſigned

figned to their Correfpondents in Europe.
But though the produce was confiderable
for this Colony, it bore a very fmall proportion to that of the Middle States : Nor
will even the quantity fhe is able to produce, be of fervice to the Weft India
Iflands, as they require chiefly flour; and
there are not mills in the Province, that
can be turned to the purpofe of making
quantities worth exportation. The Newfoundland fifhery will take off fome bread;
but befides the want of mills, Canada has
the difadvantage of contending with the inconvenience, which the fifhery fuffers from
the delay of fending veffels to fetch it.

BUT, with all the benefits to be expected
from Canada, no lafting dependence can
be placed upon it. The inhabitants are in
a difcontented ftate, and not at all averfe
to throw off our Government. They have
been kept in order merely by the ftrong
hand

hand of military power, which, whenever it is employed in Colonies at a diftance,
and more efpecially if they are of a different nation, muft have fome powerful ac-
ceffory helps, to make the inhabitants
contented and peaceable under it. Such
are thofe which the French Weft India
Iflands enjoy, where the riches they accu-
mulate from their produce, joined to the
impreffion they have of their Government
at home, keep them tolerably eafy and
quiet. We are not to infer from thence,
that the French Government is improperly
fevere; but it is a military one; a confti-
tution agreeing very ill with a Commercial
State.

GREAT expectations are formed alfo by
the noble Author from Nova-Scotia. That
this Province has a profpect of being improved, is without doubt, and fo will every
country which receives an acceffion of
people,

people, if the fubfequent meafures are
prudently taken. The number fettled and
fettling there, are very confiderable, and
there probably will be a tolerable lumber
trade in time, if the inhabitants are frugal
and induftrious; but it muft be a work of
time. And, though the noble Author of
the Obfervations has coloured too highly
the remark which he has made upon the
Territory of Penobfcot, Eaft of Cafco Bay,
its bordering fo clofely upon Nova-Scotia,
muft prove a great impediment to the eftablifhment of the lumber trade in that Colony. He tells us, " it is the fineft part
" of America for the articles in queftion,
" (mafts and lumbers) a very good fifhery,
" fine harbours, and the beft rivers along
" that coaft, which abounds with lumber
" fit for the Navy, and for private ufes,
" fufficient to fupply Britain for ages."
This does not appear to agree with his general affertion, of the want of lumber in

the

the United States, and the preference which, he fays, will be given to Canada and Nova-Scotia for thofe articles. The latter opinion is haftily adopted, without a proper attention to the fubject. The former perhaps from an indulgence of too great zeal againft the late Peace. Penobfcot is, however, finely fituated for all thefe purpofes which he mentioned. In the purchafe of neceffaries for the erection of the New Towns, and for their own maintenance, the Refugees have been obliged to apply to the people of New-England for both lumber and provifions; returning for thefe commodities the money which they brought from New-York. This is a bad beginning. They are, however, compelled by the law of neceffity, and have no other remedy than fubmiffion to it. The climate is umch againft them. The evils, however, which this produces, will be leffened, if

the

the fettlements increafe. Their fifheries in particular, have been made the object of very fanguine hopes. Nova-Scotia and St. John's appear to be well fituated for that purpofe; yet, notwithftanding the numerous Colonies which have been fent from hence, and fettled there, fully fupplied with all kinds of neceffaries, there has not been a fufficient cultivation to procure food for the inhabitants, who have been continually under the neceffity of applying to the other Colonies, for provifions for their fupport.

But it is not fituation alone that will command a beneficial Commerce. A fandy rock full of people, accuftomed to the trade they carry on, and purfuing it with activity and perfeverance, may become the feat of Commerce. This has been realized in our times, in the two little Iflands of Nantucket and Martha's

I   Vine-

Vineyard. In Nantucket, which is only twelve miles long and three miles broad, were fix thoufand inhabitants, many of them rich, having a neat town of five hundred houfes, one hundred and forty fhips, employing near two thoufand feamen, and poffeffing fifteen thoufand fheep, befides cattle and horfes. In Martha's Vineyard, which is twenty miles long and feven miles broad, were four thoufand inhabitants, three towns, a large flock of cattle, two hundred veffels, and two thoufand feamen ; each immenfely populous for their fize ; giving a full fanction to the opinion of their poffeffing all the comforts and happinefs which honeft induftry could give them. Such enjoyments produced the natural confequence, a greater increafe of people than their trade could fupport ; and obliged them, from time to time, to fend out little Colonies, from their own narrow but numerous hive. Their emigrations were chiefly

to

to the back country of the Middle and Southern States. Great numbers of them are already settled there; and have changed the bold and daring spirit of the Sailor (exploring even the South Seas in pursuit of Commerce, to pay for the manufactures which they purchased from us), to that of the mild and peaceful Farmer. Considerable settlements have been made, and the country much improved by them. But the noble Author has now changed, not only the destiny of their Colonies, but that of the Mother Country. He has assumed the wand of a powerful Genius, and like the inchantments which we meet with in the Oriental Tales, he has employed some infernal spirit to drive them from the habitations of their fathers, where they have so wonderfully flourished and increased, and planted them in Nova-Scotia, on bleak and inhospitable coasts.

It

It is indeed too much prefumption to expect to make the fisheries of Nova-Scotia, upon which the labour of two hundred years has been already fpent in vain, fuperiour to thofe of the New-England States, whether with refpect to this Nation, or to that Colony. Nor does even the noble Author feem to defire it, if we may judge from another part of his Obfervations ; viz. " that it fhould never " be the policy of England to give a par- " ticular encouragement to fedentary " fisheries, at the diftance of three thou- " fand miles, as they interfere fo much " with the fisheries carried on from the " coafts of Great Britain and Ireland." The inhabitants of New-England are at home, with every advantage that induftry and a fufficient proximity to their fisheries can give them. Thefe circumftances, put them in a far better fituation than the European Nations, who make a long

voyage

voyage before they arrive at the feat of their Commerce, and vho muſt fetch the proviſions their fiſhermen conſume, from the American States, to reap the full benefit of ſupplying their fiſheries on the cheapeſt terms. The importation of proviſions from America into our fiſheries, is of ſo much advantage to them, that it is bad policy to prohibit it. The preſent difference in the coſt of proviſions delivered in Newfoundland, is in this proportion : Four hundred pounds from America, to ſeven hundred pounds from England. So manifeſt an advantage, determined ſeveral Merchants to fit out ſhips for the purpoſe ; but permiſſion not being granted, and others in the ſame trade oppoſing it (probably from having made their purchaſes at home, or ſome other local advantages) they were obliged to give up their intentions.

If

IF we could increase our fishery, so much as to cure a sufficient stock of fish for the West India market, which has been almost wholly supplied by America, there must be some other means found out to convey it, than the circuitous voyage which the Newfoundland ships will be obliged to make to the West Indies, as they cannot procure a freight to pay their expences on their return.

SUCH of these ships as could make early voyages, in the manner that the transport of fish from thence to the West Indies is now carried on, by a few vessels in that trade, and which bring back rums in return, would produce profit to their owners. But the full supply of fish, sufficient for the West India market, in all seasons, is to be taken into consideration. The loss of time in the Winter, would put the ships out of the usual track of their employment; an inconvenience to Merchants for which

which a compenfation is not eafily to be obtained: And the want of a freight home, would make them lofe money by their voyage. We are alfo to take care, in confining the confumption of fifh in our Sugar Iflands to the produce of our own fifheries, (could even that great object be carried into excution) that the Merchants concerned in thofe fifheries have the capacity to fupply this confumption, upon equally cheap terms with other nations. Otherwife, we are only putting our hands into the pockets of our Weft India Planters, to take out money for the payment of bounties to the fifheries.

Notwithstanding that the furrender of the Illinois, and the country on the Ohio, has been much cenfured, though very undefervedly, as they were of no intrinfic value to us, had Canada and Nova-Scotia been added to them, in exchange for the poffeffion of the Newfoundland and La-

I 4 bradore

bradore fisheries, upon the terms of the Treaty of Peace of 1762, it would have proved of essential service to us. We should have had the French alone to contend with upon the terms of that Treaty, and though they carried on the trade in a more profitable manner than the English, yet there was little interference at market; their consumption being chiefly confined to their own country; whilst Great Britain almost wholly possessed the trade of Spain, Portugal, and Italy. The French derived their superiour advantage from sending out several ships together, the crews of which acted in concert; and as soon as a loading was ready, in the curing of which the whole were employed, a ship was immediately dispatched with it; by which means many of their vessels had quitted those seas, before ours were much advanced in their ladings. These advantages being now greatly

greatly increafed, we have no other refource than our natural induftry, to preferve our fifheries upon that coaft. How
far that will anfwer, when oppofed to
America, time alone can make known.
But if the New-England States increafe in
their fifheries now, with the rapidity of the
few years preceding the War, and the more
they are confined by this country in their
connexion with it, the more will their
induftry be ftimulated, all the European
Nations will be obliged to give place, and
quit that trade.

It is time to put an end to a fubject, of
which no pleafant picture can be drawn.
Till we can force Nature to make a free
and open Navigation, and to foften the
climate, we fhall not derive advantage from
Canada or Nova-Scotia, in any degree
equal to the hopes that are held out to us.
And yet this circumftance is made by the
noble

noble Author to have different effects, according to the fubject which is treated of:
When Ruffia is to be made the fubftitute
for America, in the difpofal of our manufactures, the fhutting up of the Baltic by
fix months ice, is reprefented as preven-
tive of her having fhips or failors of her
own ; but when Canada and Nova Scotia
are to be made the fubftitutes for the
States of America, the fame interruption
in their Navigation, and the country being
fix months covered with fnow, does not
hinder their becoming nurferies for fhips
and feamen. This, however, it is, according to another of the noble Writer's opinions, not political, was it poffible, to fuffer them to become ; for he tells us, that it
is not " the intereft of Great Britain to en-
" courage our remaining Colonies to build
" fhipping exceeding fifty or fixty tons," and
confequently, not to be carriers of lumber
and provifions to the Weft Indies ; which he
further

further confirms, by rejoicing, though upon the moft fallacious grounds, that " it " is furely no fmall advantage, which we " have gained by the difmemberment of " theEmpire, that we have recovered that " moft important branch of bufinefs, fhip- " building." Suppofing it to be, as he ftatesit, an advantage, it is procured in the manner many eftates are gained, by going to law for them : Purchafed at more than their worth. The oyfter we loft in the conteft, and have only the fhell for our labour.

But to return from this digreffion. Notwithftanding the ftrong affurances of the noble Author, of its appearing, as he tells us, that " without any breach of the Na- " vigation Law, and if the regulations of " the prefent Proclamation fhould remain " in force, in lefs than twelve months, " the Weft India Iflands will be fupplied
                                         " with

" with every thing wanted from thence,
" (the American States) at as eafy a rate,
" and in as great plenty as before the
" war," there is every reafon to fear, that
thofe Iflands, efpecially the Windward and
Leeward Iflands, will be ruined in an
attempt which cannot but fail of its purpofe.

THOSE two remaining Colonies are
not of fufficient confequence to induce us
to make a beginning; if by that is meant,
the being lavifh of the bounties which we
are advifed fo liberally to difpenfe, and
the laying out large fums of money in
hopes of making tolerable fettlements.
Such a meafure can never be for
productive purpofes to ourfelves; for
when it is done, and the inhabitants are
ftrong enough to govern themfelves, they
will be no longer our fubjeds; and as the
value of the country can never be an inducement to us to run into another American

rican war, if we take a civil leave of each other, it is all that we can expect.

IT is ridiculous to talk of national gratitude. No country will voluntarily become fubject to another, when they have ftrength to become their own mafters. As foon as they can protect themfelves, they neither want, nor will receive any foreign protection. It is our bufinefs to guard againft what we have fuffered on fimilar occafions. It has coft us immenfe fums of money in making Colonial Eftates. This very Colony of Nova-Scotia has been already a heavy charge to the nation, and has never yet produced any thing of value; although we are now promifed, that (with our help) it will become the granary of the Weft Indies. We purchafed the lands of the Grenades, St. Vincent, Domi-nica, and Tobago, at double their value; at almoft the ruin of Scotland, and greatly to

the

the injury of this kingdom, in the year
1772. * The recollection of thefe dear
bought Colonial purchafes, fhould make
us cautious in now laying out our money
upon new adventures of the fame kind.

THESE confiderations prompt us the
more to cultivate a good correfpondence
with thofe antient Colonies, now a powerful and numerous People, who have
been good cuftomers for our manufactures,
and who ftill continue to purchafe them of
us.

---

* The noble Writer, in his Obfervations, has attributed
this calamity (certainly through mifinformation, the fact
being fufficiently known to have no connexion with the
American Trade) to the granting long credits to America.
But it appears from the evidence of a New-England Merchant, of the firft reputation and property, before the
Houfe of Commons, in 1775, that " he thought there
" were no more failures in that trade than in any other ;
" and that he recollected but one houfe in it having ftop-
" ped payment."

us. We ſhall reap the advantages, without the charge, of ſupporting a Government over them. It is a melancholy conſideration, to mention this as an advantage.
But it is of little avail to recur to the
paſt, or to conſider how far it is (as we
have been told) holding out a premium
for Rebellion. We ſhall not at all find
our advantage, in aggrandizing any European Power in preference to the renewing our connexion with America. Reſentment will not pay our National Debt,
or recover any part of our former glory
and riches. As Canada and Nova-Scotia
appertain to us, we ought to conſider them,
with reſpect to the immediate advantage
they can be made of to us in their preſent
condition. If they cannot maintain themſelves with a little help, it would be better to give them up. When the Refugees
who are ſettling there have received every
neceſſary aſſiſtance, we ſhall be better
able

able to judge of the use of these Colonies to us. But we ought to be very complete masters of this subject, before we engage in expence. One expence draws on another, and whatever sums are given, they ought to be proportionate to the certain advantage to be derived from them; and not founded on bare affertions upon paper, of the capacity of Nova-Scotia and Canada, to supply the West Indies with lumber and provisions, and the importance of the shipping of Bermuda, to run headlong to an absurdity of conduct, increasing our own difficulties, and involving in ruin our Sugar Plantations.

The next, and very important consideration, is the trade between our West India Colonies and the American States, the settlement of which, upon the same principles, and in the same manner it was formerly carried on, is necessary to the preservation of those Colonies, as depen-

dencies

dencies upon the Crown of Great Britain. And, in confequence of a long and well-founded experience of this neceffity, the Committee of Weft India Planters and Merchants have reprefented, " that the " permiffion of American fhips as hereto- " fore, freely to bring the produce of " the American States to the Sugar Iflands, " and to take back the produce of our " Iflands in return, is obvioufly effential."

THE noble Author of the Obfervations, has treated largely on this great branch of our Trade, but not with the fobriety which becomes a fubject of fuch import-ance. The very name of Colony appears to be his averfion ; and he feems defirous of making a general maffacre of our whole fyftem of Colonization. He is continually founding an alarm, of the vaft expence of the maintenance and protection of our Weft India Iflands ; fometimes placing to

K the

the charge of our North American, at other times, to that of our Weſt India Colonies, the expences of every war for almoſt this century. If we had been without Colonies, we ſhould not have been without war. It is not difficult to find a cauſe, when Nations are diſpoſed for hoſtilities. An affront to a favourite Miniſter in the laſt century, effected it equally well, as the paſſing a boundary line in the uninhabited parts of North America in this, or the taking a few merchant ſhips in the Weſt Indies.

IF we except our wild ſchemes of ſettling the ceded Iſlands, the returns from our former Plantations, have been much more than proportionate to the expences of making them. They have been abundant. Whenever the produce of Plantations exceeds the expence of cultivating them, they become advantageous to the State ;

State; the difference being fo much actual profit, exclufive of the benefits derived
from the navigation. On the contrary,
when Plantations (fuch as Nova-Scotia) do
not repay the expence of fettling them; or,
after long flourifhing, are, through the
mifmanagement of the Government at
home, reduced in fuch a manner as to exceed this difference (which the Weft India
Iflands will be fubject to, if the United States
are not fuffered to fupply them in American fhips with lumber and provifions)
the profit is at an end, and the poffeffion of them becomes a lofs to the State.

THE reducing thefe Plantations to this
fituation, may not be the caufe of apprehenfion to thofe, whofe ears are fhut
againft every argument that does not attempt to prove, that all Colonies are injurious to the Mother Country. They do
not fcruple to affert an opinion, that it

K 2   would

would be much better to give up the Islands
themselves, than to give up their Carrying
Trade, " that alone, (they tell us) coun-
" tervailing the enormous expence of their
" protection." The Carrying Trade of
lumber and provisions between America
and the West Indies, is set down at a
high value; and it is to be presumed there
will not be found many followers of such
an opinion : Or, of the capability of the
West India Islands to make sufficient efforts to supply themselves, by fitting out
vessels in conjunction with Bermuda : At
least, without depriving their Sugar Plantations of those capitals, which are necessary for working them. In other words,
they must find capitals for their own
Plantations ; people as well as capitals for
the provision and lumber trade in Canada
and Nova-Scotia, and for both ships and
seamen, to transport them from those Colonies. It is therefore a very unjust charge
made

made upon the West India Planters, that they deserve to suffer, or to pay an extraordinary price, if they do not make efforts which must destroy them. But another option is given them, that of supplying themselves in foreign free ports. To free ports of our own, the noble Writer is a great enemy; considering their establishment to be equal to the abandonment of our Islands. In this he differs very widely from the practice of the sagacious Republic of Holland, and from the wise commercial system, adopted at the time Jamaica and Dominica were made free ports; the advantages of which were found to be so great, that it was in contemplation to extend them generally before the American war broke out. Such disquisitions are of very little use, perhaps of great injury. For, whilst we are debating upon the question, Whether the surrender of every Plantation is of less evil than the admission of American ships

K 3

into

into the Weſt Indies, the French are milking the cow, and profiting by our blunders.

ANOTHER apprehenſion, equally ill founded, ariſes from a fear, that the admiſſion of American ſhips may be the means of affording facility to the Planter to cheat his creditors in Europe, by running away with property which ought to be ſent home to pay his debts. And we are informed, " that the evil might not reſt " here, as the North American Merchant " would be furniſhed with a valuable com " modity, which would eſtabliſh his cre " dit in Europe, and enable him to pur " chaſe foreign manufactures." The Merchants in England are in a very deſperate ſituation, if this prohibition is thought neceſſary for their ſecurity, to prevent ſuch deſigns in the Planters. They are very fully aware, that if a Planter has

any

any intention to be a rogue, he will not ftand in need of an American fhip to aſſiſt his iniquity; and that except this North American Merchant could, like the receiver of ftolen goods, purchafe the commodities at half price, he muſt be ruined by carrying it on as a trade.

IT is rather an extraordinary argument, to confider the expenfive manner in which the Planters live amongſt us, to be productive of the high price of their commodities at our market. The caufe may be eafily found for this, as well as every other branch of Commerce, where the confumption is equal to the importation; of courfe in conftant demand. No article has varied more in price than fugar, owing entirely to the briſkneſs or flackneſs of the market for it. If our confumption fhould not equal our import, then, and not before, will the price fall, both in the

K 4   Iflands

Iflands and at home; and the Merchant muft feek for a market elfewhere.

RULES may be prefcribed for having (as we are told) " our fhips go out full, and " return fo'; and that fuch is the pro- " portion, between the provifions and ftores " neceffary for the Weft India Iflands, and " their produce, that it might be managed " partly by a direct, and partly by a cir- " cuitous trade; but this object has been " greatly neglected. Britifh fhips often " went out in ballaft, often not half loaded, " and often returned with half a load." The beft prefcribers of rules, are the ma- nagers of this bufinefs, the Weft India Merchants; whofe perfpicuity and activi- ty, fupported by the beft of all arguments, great acquired property, and the profpe- rity of this branch of Commerce before the American war, prove their judgment in this Trade. Yet thefe Gentlemen have

not

not the art of carrying into practice, what is here fo very readily marked out for them. The general progreffion of this branch of Commerce, was a fhort loading outwards, and a full one on the return of the fhips. Bad crops fometimes occafioned the arrival of veffels half loaded ; but this was accidental, and a calamity to which all countries are fubject.

WE will not enter into an argument, whether it will be more for our advantage to procure Weft India produce cheaper from other nations. It will be fully fufficient to offer to the national confideration, as a full anfwer, the ample benefits which we derive from our Sugar Plantations; their immenfe confumption of our manufactures, their great increafe, the fhipping which they make ufe of, the number of faiiors employed in them, and the abundant produce which is brought to Great Britain, greatly enriching

enriching the Revenue, the Merchant, and directly or indirectly, every order of the State.

THE value of the provisions sent from Great Britain to our West India Islands, was very trifling. By the information given in evidence before the House of Commons, thirteen thousand quarters of pease and beans, and nineteen thousand quarters of oats, together with a few herrings and pilchards, were the supplies of provisions exported from Great Britain to the Sugar Colonies, in three years before the war; being upon an average about ten thousand quarters of pease, beans, and oats, each year. Salted provisions were sent from Ireland, and in great quantities. These comprehended the whole importation of the necessaries of life from Europe. The remainder of the consumption was supplied by America.

CONFINING

CONFINING this supply to Great Britain, is what the noble Author states as a great national advantage. It is, he says, " a fortunate circumstance, arising from " the Independence of America, that the " British Isles will regain, in a considerable " degree, the supply of our West India " Islands with bread and flour." But wherein this advantage consists, remains to be proved. It has one stubborn principle to contend with, which is generally considered as incontrovertible; that the cheaper a Plantation is supplied with provisions and other necessaries, the greater benefit will be derived from it. This supply in the West Indies, by America, was generally at little more than half the price they could be supplied at from Great Britain. Though the ports are now shut by law, yet they are open by evasion;* a

strong

* Lumber and provisions, in American ships, have been *actually* admitted in our West India Islands since Christmas.

ſtrong evidence of their preferring the riſque of ſeizure, to a dependence upon, and to the chance of, Britiſh ſupplies.

THIS ſupply of proviſions conſiſted chiefly of flour, rice, Indian-corn, biſcuit, ſheep, hogs, poultry, and ſome live cattle, (a great part of the laſt come from Porto Rico) hams, butter, ſalted beef, pork, and ſalted fiſh, in very great quantities, and of great value ; likewiſe ſalt from ſome of the ſmaller Weſt Indian Iſlands, the Americans being the carriers. The ſupply from America, beſides proviſion, conſiſted of lumber, boards, joiſts, planks, and ſtaves ; of oil, horſes, tallow, leather, tobacco, pitch, tar, turpentine, iron, ſloop and boat timbers, and other articles. Not leſs than one hundred thouſand caſks and puncheons were, in a year, made in Jamaica, from American ſtaves and heading. The different towns, and the buildings of
moſt

moſt of the ſettlements upon the ſea coaſts
of that Iſland, are built with timber imported from North America. The ſame
uſe of theſe articles, and many of them in
a greater proportion, prevailed in the other
Sugar Iſlands. *

In payment for theſe goods, the Americans formerly received the products of
the Sugar Iſlands, of almoſt every kind ;
of brown ſugars to a very large amount ; of
refined ſugar, ſent from Great Britain, to a
great value ; of rum very large quantities,
which was not ſaleable at any other
market ; likewiſe melaſſes, ſyrups, pannels,

coffee,

---

* Mr. Edwards, in his late Thoughts on the
Connexion between America and the Weſt Indies,
makes the whole value of American commodities
imported into the Sugar Iſlands, to amount to
750,000l. ſterling.

coffee, ginger, and piemento.* The Weſt Indians place a dependence upon the ſale of theſe commodities, and will ſuffer extremely if it is loſt to them.

Tиıs will probably be the caſe with ſugar, as the Americans can ſupply themſelves

* It is very difficult to procure the amount of the exports from our Iſlands to America, the Cuſtom-houſe books being very incorrect ; as the maſters of veſſels never enter the exact quantity, making out a looſe manifeſt before they load. The quantity of ſugar mentioned by Mr. Walker, of 25000 hogſ-heads, exported to North America, ſeems to be too much ; whilſt that of Mr. Edwards appears to be too little. But the latter at the ſame time ſpeaks of the deficiency of the Cuſtom-houſe books, re-marking, that, in a repreſentation to the Lords of Trade, Governor Littleton obſerves, that there was not *one half* of the produce entered for exportation in the Cuſtom-houſe books at Jamaica, which were actually ſhipped.

felves much cheaper at Cape Nichola
Mole, or in any of the other French ports ;
which, though not avowedly opened, yet
are fo in fact, both to import all kinds of
lumber and provifions, and to export produce in return, for the purpofe of encouraging the trade of the United States.
They may alfo fupply themfelves in the
Dutch and Danifh ports, where they will
find marts common to all nations, for Dutch,
French, and Danifh fugars; and thefe of better quality, and very confiderably cheaper
than Englifh. But fuppofing, as many have
done, that no European Nation will fuffer
the Americans to carry off their produce,
the climate of that country is fufficiently
favourable to fupply them with a tolerable
good fugar. Light as the fugar produced
from the maple tree is fpoken of, it is not
the firft time that neceffity has made a
worfe fubftitute acceptable. Maple fugar
is made in great quantities in the State of
New-

New-York; particularly upon the higher parts of the River Hudfon, and in the whole country about the Mohawk River. Some tenants of General Schuyler made as much as two thoufand pounds weight each upon their farms, and thofe fmall ones, during the laft year, which fold at about the fame price as coarfe brown fugar. Brandy, which, independently of what they can make themfelves, they have imported in great quantities, of French produce, has greatly, and will (together with their own diftilleries, which very much increafe) in time fupply, almoft wholly, the place of rum. Our Weft India Iflands cannot fubfift without their lumber and provifions; for which, without a ftipulation on our part, inftead of bartering produce, they muft pay in fpecie. It is not difficult to forefee the fituation to which they would be reduced by fuch a Commerce.

In

In the article of falt provifions, though the principal import is from Ireland, and which in quality (at leaft in moft branches of this trade) exceeds all others, and will, fo long as that is the cafe, command a pre-ference ; yet it is not a fufficient fupply. The greater cheapnefs of the American provifions, and the promixity of that coun-try to the Weft Indies, will always be the means of a confiderable fale. Improve-ments in falting will in all probability be made ; the Americans having already fent perfons to Cork to attend the methods in ufe at that place. American pork is now equal, if not fuperiour in quality to the Irifh, and much cheaper. Beef is inferiour ; but owing alone to bad management in falting; the fact having been eftablifhed, that beef, falted in America by Irifhmen ufed to this bufinefs, is equal in every quality to the beft Irifh. Before the war, fhips bound to thofe parts (now the United States) where

L   provifions

provifions were falted, were frequently accuftomed to lay in a ftock for the outward
voyage only, leaving the fupply of the in-
ward voyage to be made in America. The
great fertility of the back Country of
the Southern States, where innumerable
herds of cattle graze in the favannahs
during their mild winters, will produce
in confequence cheapnefs and plenty ; and
will in future times render falted provifions
a very great article of their Commerce.
It is want of practice (the fame thing
happens in England) that prevents their
falted provifions from keeping as well as
the Irifh.

THE great deficiency of timber in the
American States has been held out to us ;
but for what purpofe, it is not eafy to be
underftood. If it was a fact, and that
Canada and Nova-Scotia could fupply the
Weft Indies, the Trade would find its own
courfe,

courfe, and the noble Author might have
_fpared himfelf the apprehenfions of the
States of America fupplying the Weft
India Iflands. Happily for thofe Iflands,
however, there is no deficiency of timber
in America. Such an opinion can only
arife from thofe who, finding the country
round the great towns cleared of wood,
and the price of courfe dearer, have either
too much indolence; or too little judgment,
to make any farther obfervation ; and
therefore fuppofe that all the reft of America is equally cleared. There is a fufficien-
cy in that country, on the Creeks, in all
the States, to laft for ages ; and it may
be cut down on the water fide, and immediately laden in the fmall veffels which
carry on that trade. Surely our former
experience muft have told us, that lumber
was procured in fufficient quantities, and
at a cheap price in general, for the ufe
of the Planter. If the price varied, it

L 2   was

was accidental, according to the number of veſſels which arrived in the Weſt Indies; a circumſtance to which all Commerce is ſubject.

THE advantages in ſending ſmall veſſels to load lumber, militate ſo much againſt our ſupplying the Sugar Colonies in Britiſh veſſels, as to put it out of the power of a Merchant to purſue it, otherwiſe than to his ruin. The Americans will trade from their Creeks with little expence, and without delay. Our large Weſt India ſhips muſt proceed directly to the great ports, and purchaſe lumber, under the accumulated weight of tranſportation and ſtoreing; they muſt lie a conſiderable time loading, under great charges of wages and proviſions, of courſe enhancing the price of freight; and on their arrival in the Weſt Indies, they have another, and a very

conſiderable

confiderable freight to pay for droghers, or
fmall craft, to carry the lumber and provifions to the feveral ports of the different
Iflands, where the American veffels land
them without difficulty ; the whole of
which muft ultimately fall upon the Planter, who is the purchafer.

THIS mode of carrying on the Lumber
Trade to the Weft Indies, has never been
practifed but by a few opulent Merchants,
poffeffors of great eftates in the Weft Indies ; who, preferring the regularity of
fupply, though at an increafed expence,
to the leaving to their Agents the care of
furnifhing their Plantations, were accuftomed to fend fuch of their veffels as arrived
very early at home, for this purpofe. But
no one ever attempted it with a view to profit, or even making a freight for their veffels,
though they go out half-loaded. The

trade

trade could not afford it. There are some
seafons in the year, the hurricane months,
in which lumber is rather fcarce and
dear; but the Planters, in general, are
not provident enough to lay in fufficient
ftock for a day of want. Even at the period from which all our knowledge is
drawn, from that before the war, lumber,
when well chofen, was always in fufficient
demand to procure freight for thofe fhips
which were built in America, and fent to
the Weft Indies, for the purpofe of procuring a loading of fugars for Great Britain. The mafter of the veffel made his
bargain, to fell the Planter a certain quantity of lumber, for every hogfhead of fugar he would engage to put on board
his fhip. Such circumftances happened in
the time of regular fupply; how much
greater inconvenience muft then accrue
from the fcanty fupply of Britifh fhips.
For either the Weft Indians muft carry on

that

that trade with veffels of their own, or we muft do it with Britifh fhips. The poffibility of Bermuda doing it, a circum-ftance that has been urged, will not be admitted by any perfon converfant in the Trade. The dependence of that very Ifland for provifions muft be upon America. And if they could do it, another queftion arifes, Will the Americans fuffer them?

If we expect fuch great docility in thofe States, we have not profited by our expe-rience. There is one plain road, if we have the good fenfe to follow it. The advantages which we formerly derived from the Americans, when our fellow-fubjects, will be continued to us, in a greater or lefs degree, as the connexion is greater or lefs between us. If we are directed by a falfe and narrow policy, and have fo little wifdom as to think the Weft India Colo-nies will be fatisfied, fhould we tell them,

L 4   with

with the noble Author, " We thank you
" for your liberality in giving up your
" ufual method of fupply of lumber 'and
" provifions. We will make amends to
" you for confining their tranfport to Bri-
" tifh fhips, by permitting you to fell
" your rums in the American States. It
" will be of much greater benefit to you,"
we fhall add to their opinion of our folly,
the refentment of the Planters, for this
contemptuous treatment. They will naturally afk us, if we had obtained permiffion of the United States, to fuffer rums
to be imported into their dominions. In
an affair that has a relation to two different Nations, the confent of both is requifite. America has certainly no right
to queftion the propriety of any regulations which we think proper to make.
But fhe would undoubtedly make regulations
of her own, to counteract thofe which fhe
thought difadvantageous to her. What-

ever " confidence (as we are told) the
" Citizens of thofe States may be defirous
" to place in the Britifh Merchants," the
regulations of their Government being fatisfactory, would be the inducement for
them to beftow it. And though a few
veffels may be fitting out in the River, and
at Jamaica, for the American Trade, they
cannot ftir, till America gives them leave.

Upon the whole, if we exclude the veffels of the United States from our Weft
India Iflands, we muft undertake that trade
ourfelves. There is no alternative. It was
formerly attempted in the Weft Indies, but
without fuccefs. A few particular fhips arriving early at home, may, as has been mentioned, be difpatched in July or Auguft; but
the circumftances of the trade not fuffering
them in general, to depart till late in the year,
our conduct muft be regulated by this general
ftate of our trade, not by fuch partial inftances.
It is poffible to difcharge, refit, load, and fend
a veffel

a veſſel to ſea in four days, which is not commonly done in leſs than four weeks, and ſometimes in not leſs than four months. But we muſt govern ourſelves by the uſual practice of Trade, not by the utmoſt poſſible exertion which can on particular occaſions be made in it. The conſequences therefore reſpecting our ſhipping will be theſe that follow: There are very few veſſels in the Weſt India Trade, that can be ready to proceed to ſea before the month of October. To go to Nova-Scotia or Canada, at that time, is impoſſible. To go to any American port to the Northward of Carolina, is attended with riſque. There are very ſevere gales of wind in the months of November and December, upon the American coaſts, expoſing every ſhip which approaches them, to certain damage; often driving them off the coaſt, and putting them under the neceſſity of going to the Weſt Indies. Of theſe accidents, the inſtances

are

are very common, and fuch muft always
be the cafe, while the fhips, not being
ready till late in the year, a few days de-
tention by contrary winds in the Englifh
ports (to which they are conftantly liable)
muft nearly ruin their voyage. The delay of loading in the great ports, and the
dearnefs of purchafe, have been mentioned.
No calculation, with any degree of certainty, can be made of their arrival in the
Weft Indies, and of the Mafters being
ready to enter upon the bufinefs of loading their fhips, till March or April, at
the earlieft period ; a time when that
bufinefs is very far advanced in the Weft
Indies, and many fhips nearly, if not fully
laden. The hurricane months foon ap-
proaching, the veffels muft return in that
feafon, fubject to additional infurance, and
to an extraordinary expence, from the damage received during the voyage ; a
misfortune which Owners of fhips and

Under-

Underwriters, from frequent losses, are both very feelingly acquainted with; for the Merchants, on these occasions, often meet with great difficulty in making insurance, and very high premiums are frequently given. A vessel arriving at home so late in the year, cannot be ready to proceed upon the same circuitous voyage of taking in a freight of lumber by the way, until the Spring following. Thus a West India ship, which now generally performs her voyage in twelve months, quietly and with little risque, will be put quite out of her usual track.

The freight made by a West India ship to the Sugar Islands, is trifling. She depends for profit upon the freight home from thence. In three years she now makes three of these freights, and the insurance during that time, at two per cent. out, and two per cent home, is twelve pounds per cent.

cent. On the contrary, if she proceeds to North America for lumber, she will in all probability make no freight out to that country, as the ships, necessarily upon the Trade between Great Britain and America, are sufficient to carry the goods exported from hence. The cargo of lumber, purchased at a high price, will make but a small sum for freight to the West Indies. She will perform these voyages with difficulty, and with great danger and expence, and will make but two freights from the West Indies home in three years; during which time the insurance, admitting that she makes one voyage in the hurricane season, and the other before it, will be sixteen pounds ten shillings per cent. at the least, and subject to the alarms, which Underwriters are liable to at that time of the year. The present regularity of trade, which is essential in the West India Commerce, will be totally destroyed.

The

The Planters will be at one time in abſolute want of food and neceſſaries, with their Plantations ſo full of their produce, as not to have warehouſes ſufficient to place them in ; the ſhips being uſually a conſiderable time loading, which affords them great convenience in that reſpect, by taking in their ſugars from time to time. At other times, all will be hurry and confuſion, and lumber either ſelling for nothing, or no places to be procured for ſtoreing it. Every inconvenience ariſing from theſe circumſtances being now prevented, by the continual arrivals from North America, and the regularity of our ſhips carrying away the produce of the Weſt Indies.

It has been aſked by the noble Lord, how did theſe Weſt India Colonies ſubſiſt during the war, *when " even Canada and " Nova-Scotia,* any more than England " and

" and Ireland, were not open to them,
" without great expence and rifque ?"
To this queftion it is to be anfwered, that
the greater part of the Windward and
Leeward Iflands were in poffeffion of the
French; and that the three which remained
in our hands, were frequently reduced to
great diftrefs. The Planters in fome of them
compromifed the labour of their flaves for
a flender daily food. The fituation of
Bermuda was fo deplorable, that fome of
the pooreft inhabitants were actually fa-
mifhed; and it was owing to the humanity
of the Americans, who fuffered them, upon
their application, to fupply themfelves
with provifions from their States; (from
Delaware, and Connecticut in particular)
that the whole people did not perifh for
want. Jamaica having many unoccupied
lands, employed fome of them for the purpofe of partial fupply. This circumftance
has produced a landed intereft there;
which

which, though a very fmall proportionate part of that Ifland and of our other Sugar Colonies inclufively, affumes to itfelf a confequence, fufficient to make an oppofition, (the only one) to the former beneficial method of fupply from America. This plain ftate of facts demonftrates the fallacy of the affertion, " That the experience of " the laft eight years has proved, incon- " teftably, how little neceffary the Ame- " rican States are to our Iflands."

THEIR chief dependence at that time was upon England, but that often failing, they were obliged to neglect their produce, to prevent the danger of a total want of the neceffaries of life; and accordingly raifed a much greater quantity of them, than they had ever before done. Whenever diftrefs preffed very clofely upon them, they purchafed in the Neutral Iflands at a high price. But all thefe
supplies

supplies were procured upon such expensive terms, that had it not been for the enormous prices which they procured in England for their produce, the West Indies would have been ruined. This was, however, a severe tax upon the Mother Country, whose Revenues were at the same time greatly impaired by the short importations. It was an abridgement of the comforts of the People, as they were not able to supply themselves as formerly; for in all cases where the price is high, the consumption will generally be reduced in some degree of adequate proportion. During the war, the neat monies received by the Planters, for the sugars they were able to send to market, notwithstanding the high price of freight and insurance, greatly exceeded the times of peace during several years preceding the war. But we are not to infer from thence, that the profits on the whole were equal; because

M the

the quantity of the produce was greatly
leſſened. It is mentioned merely to ſhew,
that by the method of our ſupplying the
Weſt India Iſlands with proviſions and
lumber (hoops, which are light, and fill
up ſpaces in ſhips where nothing elſe can
can be put, is almoſt the only lumber ſent
from hence) the grievance, ſo far as regards thoſe articles, will be equally great
as it was during the war; for whatever
expence and riſque we are at in procuring
them (and if America ſhould ſhut up their
ports, we muſt purchaſe in the Baltic) the
burthen will fall upon the Planter, whoſe
produce now ſells at one half of the groſs
price it did in the war; and yet the principal part, ſugar, is ſubject to an additional duty of above ſix ſhillings the hundred weight.

WHATEVER may be the motive or cauſe,
moſt probably through miſinformation,

the

the very commodities formerly fent from America to the Weft Indies, are now fet before the Public in a very falfe light, both as to quantity and value. Rice, in particular, is mentioned as a mere bagatelle; yet not lefs than twenty thoufand barrels were annually fent from Carolina and Georgia to the Weft Indies. Other articles are fpoken of in the fame manner, and provifions and neceffaries made to grow in thofe Iflands in the moft eafy manner, upon paper. If a Gentleman prefers employing manufacturers in his own houfe to make the neceffaries for his ufe, it will not be denied that they coft more than purchafing of the fhop-keeper. It is exactly the fame with the Planter, who employs his negroes in raifing provifions, when he can employ them much more profitably in making fugar.

It was not by fuch means that the Weft India Iflands became opulent, and en-

riched

riched the Mother Country with their produce; a monopoly which the high price it
fells for in this country will (fo long as it
lafts) fecure to us; and makes us fmile at the
fears of thofe uninformed men, who firft
acknowledge themfelves, that the price of
our Weft India produce in the Iflands exceeds that of any other nation, and then
exprefs their fears, left the Americans
fhould carry off our Weft India produce to
other ports; though there is not, nor can
be, by their own evidence, a market in
Europe where it will fetch the prime coft.
How the Planters are to ufe the indirect
advantages which are given to them, from
an intercourfe with the world in general, is
a tale yet to be told. We fhould not fuppofe
they could, to judge from the noble Writer's own words, which are ftrictly true ;
though they do not appear to agree with
other parts of his Work, where he is full of
apprehenfions, that the Americans will become

come the carriers of our fugars to foreign
countries. He fays in this place, " That
" the difference of price between French,
" Danifh, and Dutch, and Britifh Weft
" India fugars, was fo great, that nearly
" half the fugar regularly entered, came
" from the foreign iflands, and was
" cheaper, notwithftanding the duty of
" five fhillings per hundred on foreign
" fugars." " It feems, that our fugars
" would not have been taken, but through
" the advantage of barter." Yet in a Note
to this very article he fays, " It is clear
" from this, that our fugars will not be
" taken for confumption in the American
" States, and they only mean to be car-
" riers elfewhere, if permitted to go to our
" Iflands." And again, " That the Weft
" India Planters would derive advantage in
" their principal ftaple fugar, from the
" fhipping of the American States being
" permitted to carry their produce to any

M 3   " part

" part of the world, is very doubtful. It
" is univerſally allowed, that they cannot
" afford it on the ſpot, at the price that
" foreigners can." Such contradictions
are not to be reconciled.

We perfectly agree in the opinion, that
the Weſt India Merchants are too liberal
minded men, to deſire private advantages,
that are not public benefits. But thoſe
Gentlemen muſt be at a loſs to diſcover,
(as the noble Author ſtates it) the motives of
this call upon their liberality. It does not
appear, that any uſe could be made of a
free permiſſion (ſhould it be granted) to
export their produce to foreign parts in
American ſhips; ſince no American Merchant could purchaſe, or any Weſt India
Planter export ſugars, without a certain
loſs in the ſale at any European port. Or
how the price in the Plantations could be
increaſed to their benefit, when the preſent
price

price is already a prohibition of export to any place but Great Britain.

MUCH more is to be feared from the paying in bullion for the commodities imported from America; a trade that is indisputably to the prejudice of the country which is obliged to submit to it. It will be a serious matter to the Planter, when he casts an anxious eye over the rums in his stores, (which he cannot sell in Great Britain, and therefore they will produce no advantage to the Revenue) to behold their continual waste; and to find himself under the necessity of giving up this profitable branch of his produce, whilst he is compelled to open his purse, and pay in ready money for the necessaries which he has purchased.

IT will be an equally serious consideration to him, to be bereaved of the comfort of

M 4

fresh

frefh provifions in that unhealthy climate. And both unpleafant and offenfive to be thus deprived of the fatisfaction he derived from the almoft daily arrivals of American fhips, with cattle, poultry, and many other re-frefhing fupplies for the table. Nothing tends more to the alienation of the affec-tions of fubjects, than to deprive them of the conveniences and comforts of life. The next ftep to lofing their affections, is to lofe their allegiance.

If thefe reafons are not fufficient to overcome our prejudices, will the conduct of France, a country formerly greatly infe-riour to this nation in all commercial regulations, have any weight with us? The French Colonies have people, unoc-cupied lands, and many other conveni-ences of fupply within themfelves, in a much greater degree than any of our Iflands. Yet France, fenfible of the im-portance of the neighbourhood of Ame-

rica

rica for supply, has opened (whether by an exprefs law, or by an obscure Proclamation, is a needlefs diftinction) ports in her Weft Indies for the importation of lumber and provifions from the United States, in American fhips; and fuffers them to take the produce of their Colonies in return, in fuch quantities, that the pricesof fugars in the French Iflands are greatly advanced.

No other conclufion can be drawn from the preceding Confiderations, which are founded upon the evidence of the moft fenfible and informed men, thoroughly converfant in the Weft India Trade, than that, if the Letter of the Act of Navigation is ftrictly preferved (American fhips at this time not being within the defcription of Britifh) we muft prepare ourfelves for the worft confequences that can happen to our Sugar Colonies. They will be in an infinitely worfe fituation than
they

they were during the war. At that time, though they bought their neceffaries dear, they fold their produce at a very high price. They will now purchafe thofe neceffaries at a high price, and fell their produce at a low one. In the former fituation, they were gradually declining; in this, they will fall into a rapid decay: And there is not more proper words to convey an opinion on this fubject, if the Trade between America and the Weft Indies is not fuffered to remain in its old fituation, than thofe of the noble Author of the Obfervations; who fays, " 'The delufion " will amount to that degree of infatua " tion, which hurries on the devoted to " deftruction."

A very full ftate of the Trade between Great Britain and America has been already given. It fhews the importance of that country to Great Britain; the dependence which our Weft India Iflands have

have upon it; the incapacity of the Colonies of Canada and Nova-Scotia to supply its place; and that nothing lefs than a renewal of the former Commercial Syftem will raife this Nation to the power and riches which it poffeffed before the war.

AN opinion has been very rafhly inculcated amongft us, not only by the noble Author of the Obfervations on the Commerce of the American States, but by many others, that America, by becoming an Independent Sovereignty, partakes fo fully of the nature of a Foreign State, that we cannot confider her in any other view. The refpect that is due to many worthy men who fupport this opinion, will not fuffer us to affign other motives for it, than thofe which proceed from a perfuafion of its advantage to this country. But, though thefe motives may have influenced their conduct, very different ones have actuated other perfons, who have been

bufy

buſy and forward in the promulgation of
theſe ſentiments. In ſome, it probably
proceeds from a deeply rooted ſyſtematic
animoſity, which is with them ſo power-
fully operative, that no change of ſituation could effect a change of their deſire
to reduce America to ſubmiſſion, though
at the expence of the grandeur, the power,
and even the ſafety of their own Country.
In others, from an idea, haſtily and in-
conſiderately adopted, that the ſeparation
of America from Great Britain will produce ſuch confuſion and diſtreſs in the
New States, that it will require no more
than the holding out of this threat, of conſidering her as a Foreign Nation, to induce
her to lay her Independence at our feet.

THE conduct of the former is weak,
malignant, and in obtaining the deſired
effect, would receive a juſt retribution in
their

their own deftruction. That of the latter, who, equally without ill intention, as without juft reflection, look eagerly back to our former glorious ftate of Empire before the war, is an abufe of their underftanding, which even the experience of the laft ten years cannot cure. Since, however, blindly attached they are to an opinion of the means, there is not the fmalleft probability of procuring the fuccefs which they fo anxioufly expect, from the local diffentions in America. One would think (fays the good Bifhop of St Afaph, in his excellent intended fpeech) " that there was fome Statute " Law prohibiting us, under the fevereft " penalties, to profit by experience." It fhould feem, that at leaft we are under the influence of Infatuation; the various methods which are put in practice, either by deluding us with the profpect of America's returning to our allegiance, or by

holding

holding up the great and splendid advantages which we are to derive from her being cut off from our Empire, having each their numerous and sanguine followers.

If Great Britain and America should exchange the mutual privileges which they enjoyed in their former connexion, in all cases not derogatory to the Sovereignty which we have acknowledged, and which the sensible distinction that has been made " of a people *sui generis*," strongly urges, and ought to be considered as a full answer to the plea of their being at this time a Foreign Nation, the benefit would be in a greater proportion to this kingdom, from the circumstance of its being the Mother Country. Those of the Citizens of America, who turn their eyes towards the pleasures of the Capital, and whose superfluous riches afford them the opportunity of their enjoyment, would expend

them

them in the purchase of estates in England.

THE seat of a great Empire being the centre of honours, of acquaintance with the most distinguished persons, of profitable employments, of extended Commerce, of a variety of pleasures to gratify every taste, becomes the centre of attraction to all parts of its dominions and connexions, and to the riches which are contained in them. The superfluous wealth of our dependencies, thus found its way to England. Ireland, to which, in its national situation, with respect to independence, America may be properly compared, (the difference not being very material) is a decisive proof of the advantages which this Country has derived, from the Irish participating in the enjoyment of British privileges.

It

IT is wholly immaterial to us, whether Independence was the effect of the choice of America, or whether she was compelled to it in her own defence. We have acknowledged that quality to be in her, and we must govern ourselves by the 'fact itself, and not trifle away our time in tracing out and condemning the cause of it. It is not the only Independence we have granted. It was about the same period, that we acknowledged, in effect, the Independence of Ireland. In both cases, they were extorted from us by very natural causes; the want of good Government on our part, and a sufficiency of strength on theirs, to resist us. There is no other remedy left to us, in the unfortunate situation to which we are reduced, than to make the nearest approaches in our power to the state in which the Empire was placed before the war. The nearer we can approach to this condition, the less we

shall

shall feel the ill effects of the Independence which we have been compelled to grant, and the more the wealth of the countries, with whom we have this particular connexion, increases, the more will flow into Great Britain.

THOSE who are so vehement in their opinion of the necessity of considering America as a Foreign Nation, have given us no solid ground of actual benefit which we are to derive from it. They depend upon the events which, according to their manner of reasoning, are to happen in future. Castle-building is a very pleasant operation of the mind, but it often leads it astray. They first go back to the time when the Navigation Act passed, and the arguments which were then used, and which then were most perfectly adapted to the occasion, without reflecting on the great changes which have happened in the Commercial

N   System

Syftem of Europe, fince that period; and on thofe, which the late Revolution in particular is likely to produce. They next threaten us with the refentment of Ruffia, which is held out as a bugbear to us; and then bring forward Ireland by force, to join in this ftrange combat of one of the plaineft fyftems in the world— the revival of our ancient Commercial Connexion with America.

In the firft place, the circumftances at this time, and at the paffing of the Navigation Act, are fo widely different, as not to admit any parity of reafoning upon the fubject. In the next, Ruffia is actually a rival to us in fome of our capital manufactures. In that of linen, the quantities that we import, make us feel for our own manufactures, in fuch a competitor. This they do not themfelves contradict; for we are told in the

Obfer-

Obfervations of the noble Writer, that
" if we fhould not be able to command
" the more fubftantial advantages of being
" the manufacturers (fpeaking of linen)
" ourfelves, our next object muft be that
" of endeavouring to fecure the fupply of
" the American market with thofe ar-
" ticles ;" though he furely forgets, that
the methods which he prefcribes in various
parts of his Work, will prove a very bad
medicine for curing America of the prejudices, which fhe may have taken againft
us. If he wanted to fecure fuch a trade,
cooling and lenitive draughts would have
been much more fuitable, than the rough
horfe medicines which he prefcribes. In
the manufacture of iron, he remarks himfelf, that fhe makes great quantities of
nails for home confumption, and having
" taken off the duties, may now greatly
" underfell us ;" a ftrange recommendation
of a country to fupply the deficiency in

fale

fale of the manufactures, with which we formerly fupplied America.

However, with refpect to the principal raw materials with which Ruffia fupplies us, viz. iron, and hemp, the chief articles in common to that Empire and America, if we do not think the importation, duty free, from both nations, neceffary for the encouragement of our own manufactures, as well as for the difcouragement of thofe which have grown up in the fame country with the materials, there can be no objection to the equalizing of the duties upon them. As to Ireland, there is no fmall probability (from the connexion which that country, particularly the Northern part, has with America) of her being difpofed to take the lead herfelf in this bufinefs, if we do not. There is no want of inclination, or knowledge of the advantages which fhe

will

will derive from it, to prompt her to wiſh for a Treaty that might be made, upon terms very profitable to both Countries.

THE circumſtances which attended our former Trade with America, can alone af-ford the means of properly inveſtigating the oppoſite opinions which have been given on the ſubject. They have already appeared in the courſe of this Work. They ſhall now be repeated in ſubſtance, for their better elucidation.

THERE are many important points for our conſideration. The ſale of three mil-lions of our manufactures, the probability of a very great increaſe, the making this country an entrepot for American com-modities, the ſupply of our Weſt India Plantations with lumber and other necef-faries, and of our Fiſheries of Labradore and Newfoundland with proviſions, the

N 3   Carry-

Carrying Trade in general, and the former employment of American ſhips in our Commerce.

THE great ſhare which we poſſeſſed of the Carrying Trade of other Nations, as well as of the importation of foreign goods, which the Act of Navigation permits in ſhips of the built of the country of which they are the growth, is a great and deciſive proof, that notwithſtanding the efficiency of that Act at the time in which it paſſed, it was become, with reſpect to any requiſite ſecurity in the chief parts of our Navigation, of very little force; ſince, independently of our own Carrying Trade, we had, in a great meaſure, that of other Nations. The ſecurity of an Act of Parliament, an authority in which the general Intereſt muſt combine to enforce ſtrict obedience, was ſtrengthened by ſuch an habitual ſuperiority

periority of excellence in our ſhips and ſeamen, that they commanded preference by the advantages which they held out. We muſt always acknowledge the Act of Navigation to be the excellent ſchool in which we were educated, and which protected us, in our infant ſtate, from the intruſion of our neighbours. And, although our Commerce, when it aſſumed a manly form, became ſufficiently great for its own protection, we ſtill retain every recollection of the excellence of this venerable Law, and the full remembrance of its former kindneſs in our youth.

WE muſt not at the ſame time forget, that, in this ſuperiority of our Carrying Trade, we are greatly indebted to American ſhipping. There were little leſs than four thouſand ſhips employed in our Commerce, including the Trade of America and the

Weſt

West Indies. This is an enormous gap to be filled up, and which the experience of a few years, since the breaking out of the war, has shewn us, was supplied, not by British, but by foreign ships; and which increased so much, as to form seven parts in fifteen of the shipping employed in our service.

The tonnage of the shipping employed in the Commerce of Great Britain, at the commencement of the war, has been stated to be, 1,300,000 tons. This includes all the shipping trading in and with this Country, whether built in Great Britain, its dependencies, or in Foreign Nations, bringing the produce of the growth of those Nations to Great Britain. Amongst this shipping were 398,000 tons of the built of America, now composing the United States, distributed, indiscriminately, in all parts of our Commerce.

THE

THE tonnage of fhipping at that time employed in the Thirteen States, were alfo ftated at 400,000 tons, one half of which was employed in the Trade to Europe, and chiefly belonged to Britifh Merchants, navigated by Britifh feamen, compofed of the built of Great Britain, and its dependencies, without diftinction; and for the moft part involved in the 1,300,000 tons already given in the tonnage employed in the Commerce of Great Britain. The remaining part was employed in the Fifhery, Coafting, and the Trade between America and the Weft Indies.

THE proportion of American built fhips to Britifh built, employed in the general Commerce of Great Britain, was in the fame proportion as 23 to 40 before the war; and as 11 to 35 at the peace, many being worn out during that time, and which were

not

not replaced. But as American ſhips decreaſed in numbers, Foreign ſhips increaſed; and the latter, which before the war, bore no greater proportion than 12 to 40, at the peace was as 29 to 35; which proves the deficiency not to be ſupplied by Britiſh, but by Foreign built ſhips. And if the American ſhips which remained at the peace, are to be deemed as Foreign, the proportion will then be (making the proper allowance for veſſels taken from and by the enemy during the war) in the proportion of 35 to 40; or nearly the ſame number of Foreign, as of Britiſh built ſhips.

SHOULD the deficiency be ſupplied by the Northern Nations, who build much cheaper than Great Britain, it cannot be on ſuch beneficial terms as thoſe furniſhed by America; becauſe we muſt pay for the former in ready money, the balance of

Trade

Trade being already greatly againſt us ; for the latter we ſhould make payment in manufactures. We may be deſirous, though there is very little expectation of ſeeing our deſires gratified, that the Ship-builders on the ſhores of the Baltic purchaſed a ſufficiency of our manufactures, to make them cry out, with the noble Author of the Obſervations, that they could not pay for them, without giving ſhips in exchange : But we find to our coſt, that we muſt not only pay in ſpecie for them, but ſhall alſo be obliged to give up the benefit of the Navigation of Foreign Commodities ; the loſs of which we have felt ſeverely during the war.

But ſuppoſing this loſs to be only felt for a few years, until we could extend our own Building Dock-yards, already very great, upon any tolerable terms : So long as we can barter our manufactures for

American

American ſhips, we are only, by their ex-
cluſion, giving encouragement to our Ship-
builders, in preference to the Clothier, the
Weaver, the Iron-maſter, or any other
manufacturer of goods for export. Experience has ſhewn, that the incorporation
of American ſhipping amongſt our own,
has been productive of advantage to our
Navigation ; and Britiſh built ſhips have
increaſed in number, as much as, from
the circumſtances of the increaſed price
of building, it ſeemed poſſible for them
to do. This increaſe of price has been
very great within a few years : A ſufficient
proof that we ſuſtained no injury from
the incorporation of American ſhipping,
and that we cannot preſerve the Carrying
Trade, without ſupplying the deficiency
of ſhips, on the ſame low and advantageous terms, as thoſe which made us
Maſters of it : And which, ſo far as
regards the ſhare we poſſeſſed of the Carrying

rying Trade of Foreign Nations, and the importation of Foreign Goods from the places of their growth, wholly depends upon the cheapnefs of Navigation.

As this general head of American fhips may admit of fome differencce, that country being compofed of fuch a variety of people and fituations, as not to admit the fame argument to be applied to all, a divifion fhould be made of the New-England States, from thofe to the Weftward and Southward of them; becaufe the principal fear which we are taught to apprehend, arifes from the former, they being reprefented as the only great builders of fhips, and therefore fuppofed to be in a capacity (if admitted as formerly) to prevent the ufe of Britifh built fhips. This is not ftrictly true; for of the fhips built in America, the New-England States fupplied only about three-fifths. But to take

it

it upon the largeſt ſcale, would it not be a profitable trade, to barter our manufactures for their ſhips, upon ſtipulated terms? Theſe terms ſhould be, to grant the privileges of Britiſh ſhips to ſuch of their veſſels as were purchaſed by us, or were the joint property of Britiſh ſubjects, and the Citizens of the United States; one half of which to be always the property of Britiſh ſubjects. Excluſive of the political benefits to be derived from ſo cloſe a connexion with a people of the ſame manners and language, it would inſure to us many of our manufactures, which depend upon Navigation. By this means, the American Commerce would be ſo intermingled with ours, that it would centre chiefly in Great Britain. The Carrying Trade would reſume its former advantageous ſituation, and in time of war, the United States (the locality of them in all operations of war in the Weſt Indies being of great importance) would prove particularly uſeful to us.

BUT

BUT to allow fome ground for thefe fears of the New-England fhipping; for it muft be that country from whence the chief fupply is to proceed; as the inhabitants are the principal rivals in our Fifheries, and as it is the only part of America that may be made capable, in time, of injuring us in the Carrying Trade, would it not be more prudent in us, if we could procure a fufficient fupply of fhips upon good terms from them, to get into our poffeffion fome of thefe dangerous weapons of offence; and to participate (at leaft as much as we can) in the trade which thefe States carry on, by the fupply of our manufactures for their fhips and produce? In fhort, having a full experience of the paft, and admitting the apprehenfion of future danger from the New-England States to have fome foundation, whether it is not better

" To bear thofe ills we have,

" Than fly to others which we know not of?"

THOSE

THOSE imaginary ills, for such they are; America being too much reduced to give us any present alarms of rivalship in the Carrying Trade. She is in the state to afford a gradual and useful supply, in proportion to our wants. She has as solid means within herself, as any Nation can possess, far beyond the greater part of the European Governments; and yet, with even such abilities, time is required to bring them into action. Thus far we may be assured, such is the natural force of the strong resentments which this war had caused, that the more attempts we make to depress their Commerce, the more will their wonderful industry and spirit in adventure be stimulated to revive and increase it.

But should even the Trade of the New-England States, with respect to the advantages of it to this country, be suspended

in

in a doubtful balance, that of the Middle and Southern States would however greatly preponderate in our favour. Thefe States muft depend at this time, almoft wholly upon European fhipping, for carrying off their valuable produce. They build many fhips, but they were formerly, and would again be, if we acted with any degree of prudence, equally for the account of Britifh Merchants; and they would bring from thefe States their produce to Great Britain; the payment for which would be made in manufactures directly to them. Such decifive advantages, particularly with refpect to the Carrying Trade, at the time that they fhew the propriety of our culti-vating the ftricteft union with thefe States, point out the neceffity of taking into our confideration, how far lefs advantages, or even a trade carried on without lofs, with the New-England Governments, ought to have weight with us, if fuch a beneficial

O   connexion

connexion with the other States is to be procured on no other terms.

In short, if our ships are confined to the built of these kingdoms, they will be confined to such monopolies, as we can constitute by law, and can maintain as such to the advantage of our subjects. For to contend for the Carrying Trade in general, with Nations, who can procure shipping for all the purposes of Commerce, at almost half the expence, * is to contend with impossibilities.

In

---

* Merchants of the first credit in New-England, will engage to deliver ships well built, and completely fitted for sea with the best materials, at seven pounds ten shillings per ton, and declare at the same time, that they shall make a great profit by this trade.

In the fale of our manufactures fince the Peace, there has not been that prudent management, which an affair of fuch confequence required. We have opened our ports for the exportation of goods, without a proper confideration of the manner in which the payments for them were to be made; having prohibited the importation of many articles, which would make a valuable part of them. Lumber and provifions for the Weft Indies, provifions for our fifheries, and fhips and oil for Europe, would be fufficient returns in payment for very confiderably more than one million in value of our manufactures.

FORMERLY, although the Americans received Weft India produce in barter, to the amount of about two-thirds of the commodities with which they fupplied our Iflands, and the excefs of about one-third, found its way in bills of ex-

O 2   change

exchange for the purchafe of goods; yet as they had no legal permiffion to export the articles fit for the Weft India market to any other than our Iflands, and as moft of the goods which they received in re- turn, were neceffaries for their own ufe, fome part of the produce which they fent to Great Britain to exchange for our ma- nufactures, muft have been diverted from this purpofe, for the purchafe of thofe neceffaries which they wanted in foreign parts. So that in every point of view, the exclufion of their commodities from the Weft Indies, is the exclufion of the fale of fo much of our own manufactures; or what is perhaps worfe, a deficiency, at leaft a delay in payment (the American produce having been greatly reduced by the war) for thofe manufactures with which we have fupplied them; in cafe America is not able to difpofe elfewhere of the goods which fhe offers to us in exchange. And, if fhe is able,

wherever

wherever American ſhips are, in future, ſent with cargoes, they muſt, if to be procured on tolerable terms, purchaſe goods, in preference to their veſſels returning without any freight. We therefore make our election of the riſque of receiving no payment at all, becauſe, at a future period, we may have a chance of being ſupplied with thoſe articles by our own ſhipbuilders and fiſhermen.

Our ſhipwrights, and our fiſheries, are undoubtedly of importance to us, and it is our duty to pay the utmoſt attention to their preſervation, But at the ſame time we ought not to neglect this precaution, that the hope of future advantage, by their extenſion, is not indulged at the expence of other branches of our trade, by depriving many of our manufacturers, of preſent benefit, and weakening their future proſpects. The manufacturers who have truſted

the

the merchants, and the merchants who have trufted the Americans, will find the effects of this exclufion of trade ; when at the expiration of the credit that they have given, they demand payment for the goods which they have fhipped. If America is able to pay for her imports with her produce, it is as much as fhe will be able to do at prefent. The goods, therefore, which they offer in payment, and which we refufe, may prove fo much certain lofs to ourfelves. In this view we are to confider ourfelves as proprietors of large warehoufes, full of manufactures for fale, and foliciting for cuftomers. In exchange for which we fhould refufe no commodities that can be rendered ufeful to us, either for confumption or export.

THERE is one principle, by which every Nation fhould be governed in the management of her manufactures, her plantations,

tions, and her fisheries. This is attentively to search for, and carefully to procure raw materials and provisions, upon the cheapest and lowest terms. In the supply of her manufactures, this operates in the encouragement given to the importation of raw materials. In the supply of her plantations and fisheries, with the necessaries for their use; whether manufactures, lumber, or provisions. Without these precautions, they cannot be carried on with the advantages which they are capable of receiving, and which the benefits they render to the Mother Country give them a right to enjoy.

THIS respects the fisheries chiefly in the article of provisions, for the supply of which they are now confined to Europe; consequently to a much dearer market than they could find in America. This is an object of magnitude, as we have not

O 4 only

only at this time, powerful European rivals, but a very alarming profpect in the future contention of America; and there-fore the cheaper we can render our fish for fale, the more extensive will be our fisheries, and the firmer the fecurity to this important branch of our navigation.

It refpects the Weft India Iflands in two ways, the profit attending their eftates by the cheap fupply of their ne-groes, and of other neceffaries for their Plantations; and the comforts they derive from the continual arrival of frefh pro-visions, which they cannot procure from England. The confining the importation into the Weft Indies of American com-modities, to veffels of a fpecific burthen, and reftraining the produce in return, prevents a great deal of fupply, and will not remove the jealoufies and appre-henfions which the Proclamation for re-

ftraining

ſtraining this trade, has already cauſed in
America. It appears to have little or no
advantage, and to have ſeveral miſchievous
qualities. It admits the veſſels of New-
England, from whom we derive the leſſer
benefits in our American Commerce, and
excludes great part of thoſe of the Middle
and Southern States, which are by far the
moſt profitable. If the deſign is to leave
the greater part of this trade to our large
Weſt India ſhips, it cannot be carried on
by them, from the great expence and
delay attending the voyage, and the ſmall
freight to be made by them. The reſtraining the American ſhips from taking
produce in return, is ſurely unneceſſary,
and therefore tends to excite jealouſy,
without the leaſt benefit to be obtained by
it. The advantages both in the purchaſe
and in the ſale of ſugars, can be only made
for, and in, the Engliſh market: And
therefore there can be no danger of America's

rica's carrying off any more produce, than what will merely pay for the commodities she supplies; which is much more for our advantage than paying in bullion. The West India Islands have now the privilege of exporting sugars to the Southward of Cape Finisterre; but the price is so high in the Islands, that it is, in effect, a natural prohibition.

THE benefits which will arise to this country, by making it an entrepot for American commodities, in other words, a great free port for their goods, the chief source from whence Holland has derived her immense wealth, and the example which France is now following, ought to be a principal consideration with us in the settlement of the American Commerce with this country. The same attention should be paid to the arrangement of duties on goods imported. Those articles, of

smal!

fmall consumption in this kingdom, and producing very little or no Revenue, but which are the staple of any of the States, should be imported free of duty, as the advantages arising from the transporta- tion, and the making this country an entrepot for them, is of much greater im- portance. The fame conduct should be preserved refpecting commodities which are confumed in our shipping. The con- trary would only operate as a tax upon them ; equally fo upon all articles apper- taining to the dying of manufactures ; as well as bulky wood ufed in the cabinet, joiners, and blockmakers trades, their fcarcity being now felt in the magnitude of the price,

If the Americans are to be confidered in the fame view as foreigners, the ad- ditional charges to which their shipping will be liable, and of which they now bit-
terly

terly complain, will render this plan abortive. The comparatively fmall charges in the ports of France and Holland, (in the former little more than one-third part, and in the French Weft India ports not more than one-fourth of what is paid in our Iflands) will throw the fcale greatly into their favour. If we recur to our experience, to the amazing growth of our power and riches, which kept an even pace with the growth of our Colonies, it will certainly point out to us, the fuperiour wifdom of endeavouring to recover thofe who are gone aftray from us, rather than in a fit of puerile and fruitlefs refentment, to turn Knights Errant in fearch of new confumers of our manufactures.

COMMERCE is not proof againft injury, by even temporary obftructions; but when thefe become of long continuance, its diffolution is certain, though in a gradual and imperceptible degree. Like a river,

the

the falling in of whofe high banks has obftructed its navigation, and forced its ftreams to wander through the neighbouring meadows; if the bed is not immediately cleared out, the earth, accumulating by the rubbifh which the current continually brings down, at length chokes up the paffage, and the waters, compelled to forfake its old channel, feek out a new courfe. Commerce is in a great meafure a work of chance. A fingle manufacturer, by his induftry, has been often the means of enriching an extenfive country. He makes a great fortune himfelf, excites the emulation of his neighbours, and ftimulates them by his example. Such a man formed the great ftuff manufactory of Norwich. He oppofed himfelf to the eftablifhed manufacturers of Somerfet and Devon, who had the raw materials almoft at their doors, which he was obliged to bring from a great and expenfive diftance; yet, his example being followed, Norwich

wich has, by its diligence and attention, settled extensive and useful manufactories, whilst the original workmen, flothful, and fecure in poffeffion, have gradually declined, and are now almoft funk into oblivion.

It was induftry alone which filled Briftol and Liverpool with their prefent opulent inhabitants. Probably the dread of pirates fixed them in a fituation, in all other refpects, as commercial towns, miferable. The approaches from the fea terrifying. Yet activity, which a fear of danger generally excites, at length made even thefe difficulties tolerable to them. When the greater civilization of Europe put an end to piracy, they had no other refource for the prefervation of their Commerce, than in the continuance of this activity. Thus, they acquired wealth, and forming extenfive connexions, enriched the inland country within the reach

of

of their Commerce. Briftol, finely fituated for internal fupply, has improved
the whole country upon the Rivers Se-
vern and Avon, and upon the Welfh,
Cornifh, and Devonfhire fhores. Liverpool, though not fo well fituated for extenfive fupply, has been the principal
means of eftablifhing the manufactories
of the rich town of Manchefter, a work,
which is alone fufficient to aggrandize its
name.

THESE digreffions, though they lead
from the immediate fubject before us, yet
have a connexion with, and are ufeful in
the confideration of it. They teach us,
that Commerce will wander from one
place to another, as particular circumftances direct it. The inftances which
have been given, are of cafual occurrences
in our own country, confequently are
not of national injury. But when we
recollect,

recollect, that almost all the manufactures of this country have been brought from the Continent by the same accidental circumstances; and that they have flourished here from the same causes, the industry and emulation of private persons, we cannot be too anxious for their preservation in their present condition, or be too careful of retaining the export of them in the channels to which they have been accustomed. Experiments are hazardous. We know not what rivals we may create, if we prevent the Americans from trading with us. A country where agriculture or fishery is the staple, and where great plenty of unoccupied and fertile lands prevent the settlement of manufactories, will prove better and more certain customers, than settled nations, whose principle is to encourage manufactories of their own.

THE

THE former narrow policy of France and Spain, in the adminiftration of their commercial concerns, for they have long ago feen the difadvantages of it, is now held out to us for imitation. The recommendation of the example of an abfolute government, always lefs favourable to Commerce than a frce State, comes with a bad grace to a people, whofe fuperiority over their neighbours has been owing to the fpirited exertions, which the freedom of their Conflitution has enabled them to make in Trade and Navigation. The obvious effects of this conduct has given a precedent, which even thofe governments have followed, and they have given proofs, France particularly, very ftrong ones, of the benefits which they have derived from it. It was a very oppofite conduct to the policy thus recommended, that put this Nation in poffeffion of her power and riches.—But abfolute Monarchies are not the countries

P

to fearch for examples of commerical regulation. It would be wifer for us to turn our
eyes to the induftrious Dutch, whofe immenfe riches fhew the advantages of the
eftablifhment of a Free Trade. Could this
country be made one great free port, the
fame confequences would follow. But
alterations of importance are, at this time,
of ferious moment in this country.

By the Treaty between France and
America, the former muft have all the
privileges of the moft favoured Nation.
The fubfequent Treaties between America
and the European Powers are upon a principle of reciprocity : An argument is
drawn from this, that as America can give
us in return no fuperiour advantages, we
are not to grant more to her than to foreign
nations. It is not fuch Treaties, it is the
probable effects of trade that ought to direct our actions. It can never be a detriment

ment to us, that France poſſeſſes the grant, when ſhe has not the means of carrying it into execution. The advantages which we enjoy, afford us the power of rendering it uſeleſs to her. France could then have no other proſpect of material advantages by the Independence of America, than what accrues to her from the diſmember-ment of our Empire, and the weakneſs to which we are in conſequence reduced. But this will be of the greateſt importance to her, and will amply indemnify her for the expences of the war, and whatever loſſes ſhe ſuſtained in the conteſt. It is very flattering to our pride, but affords no comfort to our pockets, to conſider the reſiſtance which we made to a hoſt of enemies. Our reſources went beyond the moſt ſanguine expectations. But our exertions have added above one hundred millions to our debt, and four millions per annum to our taxes.

P 2 Yet

YET we are told, that it is some satis-faction to think, " That by breaking off " rather prematurely with America, " Great Britain may find herself in a " better situation, than if she had fallen " off when more ripe." If the situation we are now in, with two hundred and forty millions of debt, affords us any satis-faction, in reflecting upon our having thus prematurely seperated from America, what must have been, by a parity of rea-soning, the consequence of the continu-ance of our former connexion. Nothing less than ruin to this country. A conse-quence, however, (which from the power and riches we enjoyed during our con-nexion with America, and which, toge-ther with our other colonial possessions, was the fountain of wealth from whence the supplies were drawn, which proved the means of creating this immense debt) few will be inclinable to allow ; or to

support

support the fallacious position from whence it is drawn.

THE establishment of a connexion between this country and America, upon terms of mutual advantage to each State, is not a matter of such difficulty as might be imagined, from the present apparent indisposition in both Nations towards it. If there is not such a stock of good temper as could be wished, it is the effect of very natural causes, which mutual good dispositions will in a little time enable each of us to remove. The English are not yet recovered from the shame of their disappointment; and though they have lost their dominions, they have not lost the recollection of their former supremacy; and expect something like the usual deference still to be paid to them. The Americans, on the contrary, having by perseverance, and through long and

P 3

painful

painful fuffering, attained to an unlooked
for Sovereignty, are naturally jealous of
the Power from whom they have wrefted
it. The more fo, as the eftablifhment of
thefe great Republics muft have been an
unexpected event to them, and of which
they could not have had the fmalleft idea
at the breaking out of the war. It was one
of thofe revolutions, marked by the fin-
gularity of the event. A part of our North
American Colonies, unconnected with
each other, by the means of Committees
of Correfpondence, formed a Congrefs of
Deputies from each Province. That Congrefs, without any preparation for war,
had the firmnefs of mind to look this
great Nation in the face, with a fixed determination to refift its power. It did not
fhrink from even the armed force, prepared
for the declared purpofe of compelling
them to fubmit to Acts of Parliament,
which had proclaimed them enemies to
the

the State, their persons liable to the pains of High Treason, and their property to Confiscation ; although the only hope they had of preserving the troops raised for their defence, rested upon our ignorance of their want of the necessary means to keep them embodied. The desperate action at Bunker's Hill, had deprived them of the little ammunition which they had been able to procure, and they were left so very destitute, that had our troops marched out of Boston, the Americans must have dispersed. Comparatively speaking, they had none, and when the sentries were relieved, their musquets were left behind upon constant duty. Till the capture of those valuable British store-ships, which were taken by the people of New-England, and which afforded the principal supply of all kinds of military stores to their Eastern army, under General Washington, they deceived both our troops and their own,

by

by the daily arrival of waggons, which were driven in great parade in fight of our works, laden with barrels, wrapped up carefully in clothes like gunpowder, though filled only with fand.

THE fame want of means appeared in the other parts of America. The Congrefs refolved upon an expedition into Canada, but were deftitute of military ftores neceffary to carry it on. In this condition they heard of an ordnance fhip being expected at St. Auguftine. The information was tranfmitted to the Executive Government of South Carolina; the Prefident of which, with a decifion equal to the importance of the occafion, iffued an order to the Commander of an armed veffel, for feizing the gunpowder on board the ftore-fhip, then lying at anchor off the Bar of St. Auguftine, waiting for water to carry her into port. This order was

in

in part executed. And the gunpowder there taken, was brought to Charleſtown, from whence it was conveyed by land carriage, from the moſt Southern Colony, through the vaſt Continent of North America, to an army acting in the moſt Northern part ; and which, without this accidental circumſtance, could not have ſtirred.

THESE extraordinary events are ſtrong proofs, that America had no intention to ſeperate from this country. But there is little need of acceſſory evidence, when we have the moſt irrefragable teſtimony in the conduct of the Congreſs itſelf. For even in the Spring of the year 1776, the Congreſs was ſo very averſe to a ſeperation from Great Britain, that, on a motion by one of its Members for a Declaration of Independence, there were not three of that ⸳ ⸳⸳ ⸳ʰᵃt could be brought to ſupport

it, nor was it fuffered even to lie upon the table. It was the circumftances of the times,
particularly the Prohibitory Act paffed in
December 1775, and the meafure of en-
gaging of the German Troops, that at laft produced it, and even then with fome difficulty, a fecond and third attempt having
failed ; and though the Declaration was
at laft carried in July 1776, it was by
management alone ; a general concurrence not being then obtained, nor till a
confiderable time after that period; the
incidents of the war ftill ftrengthening and
confirming it. Independence, in a manner,
treading upon the heels of Dependence,
and peace quickly fucceeding a civil war,
of all others the moft dreadfully fevere to
the fufferers ; it would be an example
without precedent, fhould a people, the
authors of a great Revolution, be fo little
fubject to the common paffions of mankind,

kind, as to meet fuch a turn of fortune unmoved.

THE feveral Acts of the different States, fuch as the extraordinary duty of twenty-five per cent. upon Britifh fugars in South Carolina, an additional duty upon Britifh fhips and goods in Maryland, or any fimilar Acts, muft be attributed to the caufes of refentment, which locally affected each State. Thefe caufes may be traced; particularly with refpect to the inftances which have been given. In Carolina, the people had not only fuffered the moft melancholy ravages of the war, in their perfons and eftates, but at the conclufion of it, fuftained a fevere lofs in the taking away of negroes by the Refugees, which they alledged to be the property of perfons remaining in the State, and ought to have been reftored to them. In Maryland, the Proclamation reftraining the Provifion

and

and Lumber Trade with our Weſt Indies, which was a very growing Commerce in that State, ſtrongly excited its reſentment. The more ſo, as they appeared to manifeſt a great deſire to renew their former connexion with Great Britain, by paſſing Acts of their Legiſlature for the purpoſe, immediately on the ceſſation of hoſtilities.

SEVERAL trifling and unforeſeen events had fallen out in America, which the enemies of both countries had too much ſucceſs in conſtruing into intentional inſult. At New-York, the flag of an American veſſel was forcibly hauled down by the Refugees. The Britiſh flag was treated in the ſame manner in an American port; and, as will always happen on theſe occaſions, each threw the firſt offence upon the other. Both Governments were ignorant of theſe outrages at the time they were committed; and when they came to their know-

knowledge, they declared their difapproba-
tion. They were the acts of private people, done in the heighth of refentment
and retaliation, and which neither of the
Governments could prevent.

ANY act of retaliation by a feperate
State, without the concurrence of the
fœderal Union of the whole Body reprefented in Congrefs, fhould be attributed merely to the effect of local
refentment, and ought not to be con-
f,dered by us in any other view. No
future difadvantage can arife from it, as
it muft give place to the Commercial
Treaty ; which, it is to be hoped, we
fhall earneftly endeavour to form upon a
folid and permanent foundation. For hitherto, the regulations which this Country
has made with refpect to the American
Trade, and reftraining their fhips from
entering her Weft India ports, have no
other conftruction put upon them in America, than as fo many proofs of the indif-
pofition

pofition of Great Britain towards a future connexion ; and of an improper direction of their internal commerce, by proclaiming a permiffion to Britifh fhips to enter their ports, and carry the commodities of America to our Weft Indies. We will not enter into the merits or demerits of fuch conftructions. But waving the confideration, America would have been acting with the greater dignity, and more becoming a Sovereign State, to have made its determination upon them, one folemn Act of the whole Union, to be followed by the feveral States. It appears, however, by the laft accounts from America, that all commercial regulations were, in future, to be left to the Congrefs. In the fituation of Great Britain and the United States to each other, it is very difficult, particularly in our prefent temper of mind, to prevent continual jealoufies arifing between us. On our parts, there

has

has not been an Act of a fingle State in any manner hoftile to our Trade, by making a diftinction of duties from other Nations, where our natural good fenfe (and we may venture to affert this of men of underftanding) has been fufficiently divefted of prejudice, to prevent us from a general condemnation of all the States in one mafs, and making this invidious Act a general hoftility of the whole Union.

THE diforders in America immediately after the peace, particularly when the Congrefs retired from Philadelphia, indicated a want of vigour in its Government. The confequence which many perfons in this country drew from thence, was, that this Body was not in poffeffion of an Authority, upon which any reliance could be placed by Foreign Powers; and therefore, that no Treaty of Commerce could with propriety be made, as the Government of America

America could not continue under its prefent form, but that attempts for either a
Monarchy, or the feperation of each State
from the other, forming a number of fmall
Kingdoms, or Republics, would take place;
and that, until fome fettlement of this
kind was made, great diforders would prevail; and make it probable, that our forces
then remaining in thofe States, might even
be called in to their affiftance: An idea,
in their opinion, affording very ftrong
hopes of a fecond Revolution, to the advantage of Great Britain, by the returning
Dependence of America. However chi-
merical the latter opinion might appear,
there is little doubt of its having had many
followers. It might however have been
prefumed, that fuch frequent tales of the.
fame kind, which we had been amufed
with during the war (when, amongft the
many difputes in America, no one ever
turned

turned their views to Great Britain) would from the experience of their fallacy, have fpent their force long ago ; yet at this very hour they continue to delude us.

THE other general fentiment, of a new Government not fettling without diforder, was natural to us; fince it would moft probably have been the cafe in Europe. It has happened in our own country, and men generally reafon from the experience they have of their own affairs. But the Americans having no powerful neighbours to watch opportunities of increafing their diffentions, in order to feperate and weaken them, and being in general, or the greater part, men of ftrong underftanding, plain manners, and of an active fpirit, they will be found equal to the quieting thefe dif-orders, and eftablifhing a good Govern-ment. The greateft difference of manners

Q   is

is between the New-England States, and all
the others to the Weftward or Southward
of them. Frequent marks of mutual
difguft were formerly fhewn ; unconque-
rable by any other means, than our
placing them in one common fituation of
grievance and danger, at the commencement of the war. During that period,
their mutual fafety obliged them to keep
clofely connected together. This caufe
being now at an end, the old difputes between the New-England and the other
States (there does not appear to be any
difagreement of confequence amongft the
Middle and Southern States) might poffibly
revive. But there is a circumftance that
will prevent them from arifing to any dangerous height. This, is the fettlement of
the Refugees in fuch great numbers in
Nova-Scotia, as will probably prove a
conftant check upon the New-England
States. The inveteracy, which they mu-
tually

tually poffefs to each other, will not ceafe in the prefent age. If we confider America as one Union, her conduct in fuffering fuch a number of enemies to be collected in one body, does not appear to be very good policy. At the fame time, we cannot but admire the fortuitous event, which, by bringing them fo nearly together, has removed the greateft danger that America had to fear from internal difputes.

Although the diftrefs which America felt from the ravages of the war, excited her refentment ftrongly againft this country during that period, yet it fubfided very unexpectedly at the peace. For it is owing to fubfequent circumftances, that the prefent jealoufies have in general arifen. But notwithftanding that their refentment funk towards this country, it did not at that time towards the Refugees: Although it has fince greatly abated. It is too fevere a tafk, to walk in mournful proceffion over

the

the calamitous fcenes of the late unhappy war. Every page of hiftory that treats of civil diffentions, records them as productive of the greateft cruelties and diftreffes. Like family quarrels, they are always the moft inveterate. We are therefore not to be furprized, either at the paffions of the Americans having been continually goaded by the fevere recollection of the lofs of a hufband, a wife, a parent, or a child, ftill frefh in their memories; nor at the violence of the Refugees, driven from their poffeffions, and themfelves and their families reduced to penury and want. When the Americans are fettled in peace and tranquillity, their refentments will entirely fubfide. Strong marks of this difpofition have already appeared. Many Refugees have been reftored in different parts of America. An Act has paffed the Legiflature of South Carolina, in their laft Seffion, entitled " An Act for reftoring to certain perfons

" therein

" therein mentioned, their Eſtates, both
" real and perſonal ; and for permitting
" the ſaid perſons to return to this State."
This Act extends to almoſt the whole
number, ſeperated into three claſſes.
The firſt claſs are reſtored uncondition-
ally. The ſecond upon the payment of
twelve pounds per cent. amerced upon
their Eſtates. The third are alſo ſubject
to this amercement, and are declared incapable of holding any place of profit
or truſt in the State, for ſeven years.
Such an example, and in a State which
has ſuffered ſo deeply by the war,
greatly more than any other part of
America, affords us the ſtrongeſt hope,
that it will be followed in all the States ;
and this method of claſſing the Refugees,
or diſtinctions of a ſimilar nature, will,
it is probable, be the mode adopted by
them.

Q 3 THE

THE settlement of the Constitution of Popular States, is a very arduous undertaking. The discussions of them are in large assemblies, full of a diversity of opinions, and carried on with great heat and personal warmth. Men of temper and moderation, have not, in general, so much success in opposing precipitate resolutions, as those of hasty and violent dispositions have in carrying them. When this happens, their operation upon men of the former character is in various ways. Many generate such odium by their resistance to the popular cry, that they are forcibly driven from Government. Some are displeased, and throw up the Administration in disgust. Whilst others, who have less impatience in their dispositions, submit to the violence of the storm, and preserving the possession of Government, are enabled to moderate intemperate laws, and by a prudent
dent

dent and mild use of their power, to bring the people to a proper sense of their condition.

THIS may have been in some measure applicable to America. But the disorders which they have occasioned, are now greatly composed, The best men of the several States, are, in general, in the possession of Government; and tranquillity has succeeded (even in such of them where the war raged in the greatest degree) to anarchy and distress. In the interiour parts of those States, where no Courts have sat for many years, the Judges have been perfectly well received upon their circuits; and the people were sensibly pleased with the returns of its regular Administation amongst them. In States where disputes have not subsided, such as Philadelphia, where two parties, almost equal, are opposed to each other, and are at this time discussing the Consti-

Q 4   tution

tution of Pennſylvania with heat and violence, the fœderal union does not appear to be diſturbed; ſince, in the month of January, when theſe diſputes in Philadelphia were carried to a very great length, the Congreſs at Annapolis paſſed unanimous reſolutions in affairs of the greateſt importance to the whole Union.

It has been already mentioned, that it appeared to be the intention of America to veſt all future commercial regulations in the Congreſs. This intention ſeems to be carrying into execution. The Legiſlature of South Carolina have lately paſſed the following Acts, viz. " An Act for inveſt-
" ing the United States in Congreſs aſ-
" ſembled, with a Power to levy for the
" United States, certain Duties upon Goods
" imported into this State, from any fo-
" reign Port, Iſland, or Plantation." Alſo,
" An Act to authoriſe the United States
" in

" in Congrefs affembled, to regulate Trade
" from the Britifh Weft Indies." This
fully fhews, that there is an Union for the
General Powers of Government; and that
their difputes are merely local. The diffentions in the infancy of the Roman Com-
monwealth, proved of no real injury to
it, nor in any degree impeded its growth.

But had even the greateft diforders prevailed, and a want of good Government
continued in America, it does not appear
that any benefit could have accrued to
Great Britain from this fituation of the
country. It muft be again urged, that we
are forbid by experience to expect the return of Dependence, (and in the prefent
ftate of the two countries, it is by no
means clear that we ought to hope for it)
therefore, the fooner the country is fettled
in its new Government, the fooner would
the

the trade be opened, and profitable Commerce be carried on. For this reason, the knowledge which we had of our mutual interests, should have made us early in acquiescing in all that concerned our common advantages.

THERE is a speculative opinion, formed by those persons who are pleased with exploring the future situation of an Empire, which has undergone such a mighty revolution, as to involve in some measure every Nation in Europe; that it is by no means a certainty, that the Congress will retain a permanent authority over all the States, much longer than the present exigencies require, for the composing of differences, the settlement of their debts and revenues, and the establishment of their several Governments. Whatever grounds there may have been for this opinion at the peace, when the returning dispositions of America

rica

rica appeared to carry with them every mark of a ftrong defire of reconciliation, they are now become lefs probable. For our difpofitions towards the Americans feemed to cool, in proportion as theirs warmed towards us. An apprehenfion for their general fafety appears to prevail amongft them, tending to unite them in the clofeft manner. Perhaps in future times, when the country becomes full of people, and increafes in riches and ftrength, fuch an event may happen.

In the firft place, the interefts of the feveral States, in many refpects, militate againft each other, In the next, innumerable fettlements are continually forming in the vaft countries over the mountains ; which, increafing in time, will probably erect Sovereignties of their own. Inftead of Thirteen, there may be Thirty States, or, which is very probable, and
                                    will

will therefore include their interiour fettlements, the divifions of the States which
have been mentioned in the remarks upon
the trade, may take place, and there may be
three great Republicks, according to the
fimilitude of their manners, cuftoms, and
commerce. The New-England State; may
make one. Nature has united them in
the ftrongeft manner. New-York, the
Jerfeys, Pennfylvania, Delaware, Maryland, and Virginia may form another, the
richeft and moft powerful. The third may
be the Carolinas and Georgia, nations
of planters, great confumers of manufactures, and full of luxurious produce. The
Middle States will command the great
internal Navigations, flowing through the
Hudfon and Delaware Rivers, and the
great Bay of Chefapeak, communicating
by feveral portages, with the waters of the
Ohio, and, by that means, with the whole
interiour country over the mountains. In
thefe,

thefe, and particularly in the Southern
States, are the moft fertile lands, and the
beft climate of all America; and to the
inhabitants of which, it is in our power,
by prudent conduct, to make Britifh fhips
the carriers of the manufactures of Great
Britain, and the exports of an abundant
produce in return. All our confular eftablifhments ought to be made upon this
fuppofition, as the moft natural and moft
conducive to our interefts.

IF there is any Englifhman who does
not regret the lofs of America, he does not
deferve that name ; but to fuppofe, as we
have been ferioufly told, that Independence
muft prove ruinous to America, requires
more belief than even Englifhmen themfelves, and they are not deficient in cre-
dulity, poffefs. It is too much to fuppofe,
that the fnows of Canada and Nova-Scotia
will be found fo full of temptation, as to
caufe

cause the emigration of the inhabitants of the United States; or that a six months winter will be so much preferred, as to render those fertile and beautiful countries, so widely extended at the back of the Middle and Southern States, and in which a perpetual summer reigns, deserted and desolate. The attainment of Sovereignty, by any people who have sufficient internal strength to support it, can never be injurious to themselves. The States of the Seven United Provinces were not ruined by throwing off the Government of Spain, and yet their situation was as much more precarious than America, as they were in all respects inferiour to her in power, and in future prospect. Such opinions can proceed only from a want of knowledge of the climate of the different parts of North America, and the advantages to be derived from each of them. The emigration of the New-Englanders

to

to Canada and Nova-Scotia, is not very
probable. Their emigration indeed has
been frequent ; for New-England was become fo full of people, that Colonies were
often fent from amongft them. But it
was to a beautiful Region, the back Country of the Middle and Southern States,
not to the fnows of Canada and Nova-
Scotia. If at any future period, anarchy
and confufion fhould even fo far prevail
in the United States, as to caufe the emigration of any of its inhabitants, they will
retire over the mountains, probably as far
back as the banks of the Ohio and the
Miffifippi, where numbers are already fettled.

COUNTRIES which have feverely felt
the fcourge of war, are recruited by a
very few years of peace. Flanders, which
has fo often felt it, is one of the richeft
countries in Europe. No Englifh Trader
refufes

refuses to truft a German, becaufe his
country was laid wafte in the laft, and
almoft in every continental war. America, though loaded with debt, has fufficient refources within herfelf to pay it.
The Colonies of Nova-Scotia and Canada,
which are held out to us in fo glorious a
light, will never, notwithftanding their
freedom from taxes, increafe like her States.
The fuperiour benefits to be derived from
climate, from being better peopled, and
from the poffeffion of vaft tracts of fertile
lands for new cultivation, will in a courfe
of years remove every burthen arifing from
her debts.

THE reafoning of thofe, who confider
the debt of America as fufficient to crufh
her, would have applied perfectly well
forty years ago. The infancy of a country is the time when taxes are feverely
felt. Her wonderful growth in popula-

tion

tion fince that period, has borne her up under them; and as fhe will ftill increafe both in riches and people, thefe burthens will be more eafily endured. The great danger is from the aptitude of her principal towns to run into the manners of the European Nations, and lofing that fimplicity and fpirit of frugality, which is to be found in other parts of that great Continent.

SHE is however now free from the weight of that profufion, which we felt from our former Adminiftration of America, and therefore no comparifon can, with propriety, be formed of the two Governments. Her eftablifhments are eafy to her. Every Nation in Europe folicits to partake of her Trade; and as Commercial Principles are now well known, fhe will find fufficient

markets

markets for her produce, fhould we refufe to receive it.

By ferioufly reflecting upon our own fituation, and endeavouring, difpaffionately, to repair the loffes we have fuftained, we fhall be better able to recover from them. Our fituation is bad, but not defperate. The reftoration of our Commerce muft be the means, and the only means, of the reftoration of our Power. It is an act of wildnefs and defperation, to fuppofe America loft to us, becaufe fhe is connected with France; or to reject her with horror, left fhe fhould become a rival to our Commerce; which it is our own actual intereft to fupport.

To become flaves to our prejudices, and to fuffer them to poffefs the maftery over us; to run headlong into hoftile contentions, dictated by paffion, conducted with-

out

out judgment, and producing in confequence the melancholy effects of debafing
the moft glorious Empire of modern times,
though a criminal weaknefs in a people,
has yet this plea in extenuation, that this
ill conduct was produced by the heat and
violence of refentment, at fuppofed in-
juries received. But, when fatal experience has fhewn us the confequences of
fuch hafty and ill-timed refentments, and
the bleffings of peace has afforded us the
opportunity of reafoning coolly upon our
paft conduct, furely thofe who are endeavouring, by every artful means, to keep
alive a fenfe of injury, to feed us with
the hopes of revenge, and to glut us with
the expectation of feeing thofe, whom our
arms have not been able to fubdue, either
falling a facrifice to internal divifions, or
to foreign enemies, deferve the moft fevere
reprehenfion.

To

To what other caufes than the indulgence of thefe paffions to raife our anger,
and excite our contempt, can be attributed
the introduction of fuch fubjects (continually to be met with in the Obfervations of the noble Author upon the Commerce of the American States) as the
encroachments upon our trade, the ill
conduct of the war, the miftakes in the
boundary lines at the peace, the claims
of Spain upon Louifiana, the debts of Virginia being the real caufe of hoftilities,
the advantages of the piratical States of Barbary, the want of courage in the Americans,
and the facility of reducing them by a few
ftout frigates, ftationed on their coafts. It
will not be improper to fay a few words
on thefe fubjects, the reprefentations of which
are founded either upon fallacious, nugatory, or vindictive grounds.

FOR fuch purpofes, the unaccountabl♦ affertion, that " America has robbed us of " the Export Trade of Corn, and was at- " tempting to rob us of that of building " fhips," appears to be made. The former fubject is of a very ferious nature, and obliges us to afk, whether the fupporters of it mean to arraign the Providence of God, becaufe our harvefts, in a feries of years, were not fufficiently productive to afford fuftenance to the people ; whilft America was bleffed with abundance, and like another Egypt to another Canaan, relieved us from the apprehenfion of a want of food, and from the danger of po- pular commotions to obtain by force, what the poor were not able to procure by purchafe ? Such was the fcarcity of corn in this country, at the period preceding the American war, that even the immenfe im- portations from thence proved no more than a bare fupply; and had not the abundant har-

R 3

vefts of the following years prevented the danger, which the fhutting up of the American ports would have occafioned, a famine muft have ftill enfued.

Our future poffeffion of the Export Trade of Corn, depends wholly upon our harvefts. If they are more abundant than our own fupply requires, the price of corn will be fufficiently cheap to encourage a demand for export. If they are not, we muft be contented to fuffer thofe Nations to poffefs it, who have a greater plenty.

The attempt of America to rob us of the trade of building fhips, is not eafily to be reconciled to the continual augmentation of that branch of bufinefs at home, and the confequent advance of price. The fact was, that not being able to procure a fufficient number of fhips of our own built, to anfwer the purpofes required,

America

America furnifhed us with fuch a fupply of veffels, as were wanted to maintain the Carrying Trade, which had rifen to an amazing height before the war. This very extenfive Carrying Trade could not have been fupported without this fupply. The laying hold, therefore, of this oppor-tunity to exclude the American fhipping, will not be finding the jewel of high price that we are taught to expect; but will prove, on the contrary, a fevere misfor-tune. Enough has been already faid on this fubject.

THE fuggeftion thrown out, of " the " debts of the Planters in Virginia being " a great caufe of the war," will not en-gage a moment's attention, whilft fo many real and oftenfible caufes appear. It is needlefs, therefore, to make any comment upon it. But it is very neceffary to take notice of fentiments, which ftrike at our

cha-

characters as men of humanity, in being deemed encouragers of the piratical States of Barbary. The tendency of this opinion, (at least it has the appearance of it) is to give confolation to thofe, who are enemies to a connexion between Great Britain and America, by affurances of " its not being " the intereft of the great Maritime Powers " to protect the Americans, (and there- " fore they muft fuffer) from the Barbary " States." As men who have the benefit of being taught by the mild fpirit of Chriftianity (would we were under its influence!) fuch an opinion ought to make us blufh. If we cannot hinder, we might at leaft lament the misfortunes of our fellow-creatures, who fall into the hands of thefe Barbarians. But it does not ap- pear, that America is in greater danger than thefe very Maritime Powers, who have fufficient humility to make occafional prefents, little elfe than a tribute, to pro- tect

tect their Trade from depredation. The same presents from America, it is probable, will produce the same effects. Spain is the only Nation which has exerted itself lately, in endeavours to crush these pirates by force. But the policy itself of encouraging them, from the idea of their being of use to the great Maritime Powers, in suppressing the shipping of the smaller ports, is not gaining the purpose. For even Great Britain, when she found herself distressed by having a part of her usual supply of shipping cut off by the American war, had recourse, amidst other resources, to the Portuguese and Italian States. Those very people, who are said to be the principal sufferers by the Barbary Rovers, produced numbers of ships, and supported a considerable part of our Carrying Trade.

If

IF we are speaking in the spirit of Conciliation, we may not only expect; but we must hope, that the American Character will not be a martial one. Their situation in a world of their own, their distance from European contentions, the employments of Agriculture and Commerce, which are the employments of Peace, seem to promise it. But when the idea " of the American Character not be-" ing a martial one," is taken up with contempt, when it is attended with the goading circumstance of calling the American courage in question, by transferring it wholly to their " Irish Protectors," and " to the strangely conducted war which " has been carried on ;" if those who vent these reproaches were to make trial of the American Character, they would find it pretty much the same as the rest of the world. Mankind do not greatly differ in point of courage. It might be

sup-

fuppofed, that we had fufficient experience of the folly of fuch opinions, and
how much they have already coft us.
Many certainly did not apprehend much
difficulty, in the march of a fmall body
of troops through the country; or in " a
" few ftout frigates cruizing between Ha-
" lifax and Bermuda, and between the
" latter and the Bahamas, completely com-
" manding the Commerce of this mighty
" Continent :" Yet, though they found
out their error, the fame language is again
refumed. To what purpofe are fuch hoftile
opinions refumed in this hour of peace?
To keep alive refentment, and to prepare
the Nation for another American war.
Surely the laft was a fufficient monument
of our loffes and difgrace, to make us defirous of profiting by the peace which has
followed them, and not to revive fallacious
reprefentations : Concerning which, to ufe
other words of the noble Author of the
Ob-

Obſervations, " ſuch Prophets have ſo
" much amuſed themſelves, deluding the
" unwary."

BUT it is not from words affecting the
paſſions alone, but from ſtrong incentives
to action, that we are in danger of being
drawn into diſpute. It is recommended to
the Engliſh Nation, which has found itſelf
under the neceſſity of ſurrendering up a
mighty Empire, and three millions of
people, after a bloody and expenſive conteſt, to be drawn into a new quarrel about
a few miles of Territory, in the wild parts
which form the Eaſtern Boundary, between Maſſachuſets and Nova-Scotia. If
this Territory is in the State of Maſſachuſets, which it is deſcribed to be, is not the
advice to preſerve it as a pledge, " until
" America has performed the ſeveral arti-
" cles of the Treaty on her part," an
object of ſerious conſideration to us;
when

when the confequence would moft probably be a ftimulation to the mutual refentment of the people of New-England
and the Refugees againft each other, at
this time with difficulty reftrained ? If
there had been any diftruft of the United
States not performing their part of the
Treaty, there were other more valuable
pledges than the Territory of *Paffama-*
quaddy.

IT is too ridiculous to dwell fo long on
this little Territory of Paffamaquaddy.
It would be equally ridiculous to difpute
any of the boundary lines of the immenfe Continent in the interiour parts of
North America ; which might have been
with as much reafon extended to the Lake
of the Affinipoils, as the Lake of the
Woods. Or had the American Commiffioners defired, that their boundaries
might include the Mozemleeks, the Gnac-
fitares,

fitares, the Effanapes, the Naudoweffies, the Panis, the Black and White Padoucas, the Ozages, the Great Meadows, or the Salt Rocks, our Negotiator would not have merited cenfure " for his liberality," in very civilly according to their wifhes; fince every one of thofe names are as well known in the map, as the Lake of the Woods, or the upper parts of the Miffi-fippi; and it is of as little confequence, who are to be put in poffeffion of them by the paper on which the Treaty is written. For neither of the parties have, or will have in future, any further poffeffion of of them than upon that paper. We may as well difpute about the boundary lines of fome country in the Moon, when the making of Air Balloons is fufficiently im-proved, to permit a few bodies of troops to be fent up to fight for them.

WITH

WITH the fame endeavours to prevent the ufeful connexion between us, are we made to wander through the Lakes of America, to difcover that " there is but " one mile portage between Cayahoga Ri- " ver, that empties itfelf into Lake Erie, " which *finally runs into the River St. Law-* " *rence*, and the River Mufkinghum, " which runs into the Ohio, and com- " municates with the Gulph of Mexico. " Notwithftanding the navigation of the " Rivers St. Lawrence and Miffifippi is ob- " ftructed in Winter and Spring, in the " firft by ice, and in the laft by the rapi- " dity of the waters, and notwithftand- " ing the diftance is not above fixty miles " between the navigable part of the Po- " towmack, which runs into the Chefa- " peak, and a navigable branch of the " Ohio, yet the River St. Lawrence, " (the exclufive trade of which belongs " to Great Britain) the Lakes, the Ohio, " and

" and the Miffifippi, will be the principal
" communications of the vaft country be-
" yond the mountains." The miftakes of
the portage, and the badnefs of navigation in America, which are mentioned,
are not neceffary here to be adverted to.
We are led to hope that " our Iflands,
" efpecially Jamaica, might receive fup-
" plies from the Miffifippi, whilft a cargo
" might at the proper feafon go up the
" River, *if it is open to us*, and bring lum-
" ber, cattle, mules, and fupplies of
" every kind, except fifh."—A fyftem of
trade which, it muft be acknowledged,
would be moft perfectly adapted to the
wants of our Weft India Colonies; provided—That the Cayahoga and the Mufkinghum Rivers belonged to us—That
the navigation to the St. Lawrence was
not very expenfive and full of obftructions—That the St. Lawrence itfelf was
not fhut up fix months in the year, and
that

that we had any property at all in the Miſſiſippi ; or, in the mode of expreſſion
uſed by the noble Author, *if it was open to us.*
That unfortunate monoſyllable *if*, could
it be got the better of, would make all
the difference which is ſtated in our ſituation.

It is not the wild hope of ſupplying
our Weſt India Iſlands with lumber and
proviſions from the Miſſiſippi, or any expectation of advantage to Great Britain,
or the Colonies of Nova-Scotia or Canada,
(at leaſt with many of thoſe who diſplay
this ſcene) but the proſpect which they
form in their imagination, and which they
ſuppoſe will open from the following
cauſes : From internal diſputes in the ſettlement of Colonies to the weſtward of
the mountains—from the interference of
Spain, " in (as we are told) her probable
" claim upon that part of Louiſiana given

S   " up

" up by the late Treaty," and from the production of new wars in confequence. *Divide et impera* is the malevolent principle of fome Governments. Let fuch policy be confined to Europe, where it is more known and practifed. But let a more benevolent fpeculation be made of the future profpects of the New World. We are wearied with the defolation of the rich and beautiful regions of Afia, and of the Eaft, fo full of people in ancient times, but now almoft depopulated by their ferocious Mafters. Let us at leaft have the confolation of a brighter view of the equally beautiful Region of the Weftern World, where millions of people muft, in the common courfe of human events, expand themfelves, in many places unknowing of, and unknown to Europe. In thofe fituations which approach neareft to the prefent United States, we may have the means, if we have the inclination, (but

the

the fuccefs of which will entirely depend
upon the meafures we take at this time)
of fending fupplies of our manufactures,
through the medium of the American
fea-ports. It is not therefore our intereft,
it does not become our dignity, to encourage inimical fentiments. The hap-
pier America is, the greater her wealth,
and the more extended her commerce, the
more beneficial will her connexion be with
that European Nation, which is the wifeft
to hold out her arms to receive her.

THE ceffation of hoftilities feemed to
have turned the tide of the affections of
America towards this country, notwithftanding all the calamities which fhe had
fuffered by the war. The voyages of
fhips intended for France were counter-
manded, and they entered the Britifh ports.
This difpofition continued till our Weft
India ports were fhut againft them. Many

S 2   of

of the orders for goods which were fent
to this country, were accompanied both
by produce and fpecie. It was fuppofed,
that the country was over-ftocked by European commodities, but it proved otherwife. Goods in general have fold well
in America ; and though the dearer and
leffer parts of confumption have not had
fo much encouragement, (which however
daily increafe in demand) yet the cheaper
and larger parts have fold to great profit.

THE experience of a century has (as the
noble Author ftiles it) made " the youth-
" ful ardour of grafping at the American
" Trade," grey in the employment. But
whatever affectation of youth it might
now be fuppofed to difplay on our fide,
it would neverthelefs be ftill wife in us
to run a race with any Foreign Nation,
however eager for it, fooner than lofe any
part that it is in our power to retain. If
the

the Foreigner has fuffered by his rafh and early adventures, his loffes will be our gain. But as Commerce is fluctuating, and as a firft lofs often prompts the Merchant to try a fecond adventure to repair it ; as the Poet beautifully expreffes it,

> Mox reficit rates
> Quaffas, indocilis pauperiem pati ;

We fhould not reftrain our Merchants, but do our part to open the Trade, and leave the reft to their difcretion. They are men of ability, induftry, and experience ; and if we repair the broken road, we may fafely truft the journey to their care. But if, perfifting in our former haughtinefs, we rely upon the neceffity, which we think the Americans are under of taking our manufactures, we may draw the cord too tight, and occafion its breaking in our hands, and plunging us into that mire into which our folly has led us. The Americans, in their principal towns,

S 3

are

are already relapfing into their former luxury and enjoyments. The war precluded them for a time; but a fpirit of indulgence now breaks forth, with increafed force; and the orders for goods which have been lately tranfmitted, are filled with as many fuperfluities as necef-faries. This is not a wife conduct in the infancy of a new Republick; the eftablifh-ment of which ought to be founded in examples of frugality, not of luxurious enjoyments. But if their own Governments have not this confideration, and they offer a Trade, which muft in fome meafure produce a ftate of Dependence upon Europe, it will not be a wife conduct in us to neglect fo advantageous a profpect; which will be attended with the greateft benefit to ourfelves, by difpofing of our manufactures for ufeful commodities, both for our own confumption and for export. They will, befides, come to us for ordination for their

Clergy

Clergy; for Mafters to educate their chil-
dren, and for free communication in all
thofe habits, from which the clofeft connexions are derived.

As the Definitive Treaty with America
is now figned; and the Ratifications ex-
changed; and as a Parliamentary Deliberation upon her Commerce with this Country has been too long delayed, we fhould
be vigorous in our exertions, to make
amends for our delay, and to improve the
advantages which are ftill left to us. France,
apprehenfive of them, is fully fenfible of
her danger, in the reftoration of our ancient Commercial Connexion; and no circumftance efcapes her vigilance at home,
or the vigilance of her Minifter in America, which can flatter the pride, or cherifh
the refentment of the United States againft
us. She has blinded our eyes, by avoiding
every national regulation, which fhe fuppofes would give this Country the alarm;
whilft, at the fame moment, fhe grants to

S 4   the

the Citizens of America all manner of private indulgencies. Under the conftruction of the doubtful words of a Public Proclamation, they are admitted into the French Weft India ports. And there is hardly a requeft made by an American Merchant in France, for any particular indulgence to his trade, which is not readily granted; attended, at the fame time, by perfonal attention and civilities. By thefe means, they are daily gaining the trade, and improving upon the affections of the Citizens of the United States, without exciting the leaft jealoufy in us. But this is an habitual and fuccefsful practice of the Court of France; and we are fuch a credulous people, that notwithftanding our having continually fuffered by this conduct in that Court, we never fhew, in return, any other than *a forgiving and a forgetful difpofition.* She thus fpares neither art, influence, or money, to effect her purpofes. She has Confuls, and Vice-Confuls, Agents, both

both public and private, diftributed and penfioned in every part of America. Her appointments are liberal and magnificent; whilft many of our friends in thofe States, who are at the fame time fincerely attached to the mutual interefts of both Countries, have been left without fupport.

It is not, however, difficult for us to counteract her defigns. We can do it with little trouble, and as little expence. A Minifter of good fenfe, and commercial knowledge, more eminent for a plainnefs of manners, neceffary to live in habits with a fenfible and plain people, than for the greatnefs of his birth, or the fplendour of his titles—Three Confuls for the New-England, the Middle, and the Southern States (the Conful for the Middle States to be at the fame time Conful-General) poffeffing the fame qualities, living in familiarity with the people, and judicioufly chufing the Vice-Confuls in the different

ports

ports (which would be little or no charge
to Government) would produce the effect
in a very short time, of making this Country once more the centre of American
Commerce. It is, perhaps, too early to
hope for a Treaty of Alliance. But there
must be a Treaty of Commerce, to comprehend the whole of the United States, as
one Union; otherwise the seperate Acts of
each State may tend to confusion, and be
productive of disputes. At the same time,
a plain Act of Parliament, avoiding all
manner of reference to former Acts, and en-
larged in such a manner, as to be comprehensive of the duties and regulations of the
whole Trade, should be passed. * It would
make our Laws of Trade, respecting America, familiar and easy to her Merchants,
encouraging them to form connexions with
us, which the similarity of our language
and manners would mature into a perfect
union.

Our

* The Plan of an Act of Parliament is annexed to
these Considerations.

Our interest demands that this Union
should take place with franknefs, and with
the warmeft return of ancient affection.
We have no better means of judging of the
future, than by a recollection of former
benefits.* Our habits are made to each
other. We are defcended from one common ftock ; and though unhappy difputes
have feperated us for a feafon, the day of
Reconciliation is arrived, which, we hope,
will unite us again for ever.

The clofer this Union, the greater advantages will accrue to us from it. We
have terrified ourfelves, unneceffarily, with
the fear of lofing our Act of Navigation;
a fecurity which is rendered ftill ftronger

by

---

* It is a remark which would have been made
with greater propriety in the former part of this
Work, that fuch was our Trade with America before the War, that in December 1774, fix millions
were owing from it. Yet, in December 1775, two
millions only remained ; four millions having been
remitted during that year.

by the fuperiority of our fhipping. We
are now as unneceffarily terrifying ourfelves with the apprehenfion of feeing our
Country depopulated by emigration. The
beautiful Ifland of Great Britain will never
want inhabitants, fo long as fhe poffeffes
-that wife and equal Government, which
gives fo vivifying a power to Agriculture,
Manufacture, and Commerce. When fhe
lofes this peculiar and invaluable diftinction, the emigration of her people will be very
great. But till this happens, thofe only will
emigrate, who either have not a fuffici-
ency to make them eafy, or being dif-
gufted by difappointments, are uncom-
fortable at home : Or the idle, and diffo-
lute, who are burthenfome to the com-
munity. The removal of people of thefe
defcriptions are of no injury to the State.
The firft, though in this fettled country
they are not able to provide the comforts
of life fufficiently for their families, will find
their labours attended with better fuccefs
in the New World; at the fame time, that
they

they leave room for the greater exercife of the induftry of their neighbours, by the larger fpace that is left for them. Thofe of the latter defcription can be well fpared; and from being idle drones in one country, they will be compelled to work like the induftrious bee in another, for their daily bread. Such emigrations, whilft they quicken the diligence of thofe who re- main behind, carry with them the name of Englifhmen to the remoteft parts; where the Eftates which they create, will be entailed with their language and man- ners, upon their pofterity; forming an Union that will laft for ages.

NOTHING remains, but to explain the particular motives which induced the Au- thor to intrude thefe Obfervations on the world. They arofe from a well grounded apprehenfion of the danger, which an improper refentment of the paft quarrel, and an ill-timed contempt for a future

con-

connexion with America, would probably bring upon this Nation. He does not fuppofe the fubject to be popular. But this has been the fate of every attempt to oppofe thofe meafures, which at length tore afunder with violence, the connexion which had fo long, and fo happily fubfifted between the two Countries. It was fufficient formerly to fupport an oppofition to thofe meafures, although founded upon the moft folid experience, and which have been fully verified by the event, to be deemed inimical to our own country. It is fufficient at this time, to fupport an opinion of the propriety of endeavouring to reftore this broken connexion, by thofe conciliatory means, which beft tend to regain the affections of a people, from whom we have derived, and from whom we may yet derive the moft folid benefits, to be deemed the Sacrificer of the Interefts of Great Britain to thofe of America. However laudable, however neceffary the

pur-

purfuit, there is a prejudice among us arifing from intemperate paffion, and the vexation of difappointment, that precludes, obftructs, or in fome fhape or other, ulti-mately deftroys it. The interefts of both countries are the fame. The art of man cannot devife a method of feperation, which will not be prejudicial to both. The ruin of Great Britain will materially affect America. The ruin of America will materially affect Great Britain. If fuch opinions have not the good fortune to pleafe, the Author will feel a fenfible con-cern; but having,

" Mens fibi confcia recti,"

he muft confole himfelf with the reflec-tions arifing from it. He writes only to difcover truth, which he has endeavoured to do with fidelity and attention. Others may effect it with greater ability, no one with a more fincere defire of doing good to his country.

SUCH

SUCH were the motives that actuated him in the production of this Work. It is offered with the humility which becomes an Englishman at this period, when the distresses of the Empire call for the wisdom of the wiseft, to remove them from us. If there is any thing in them contrary to the good of either country, it is most sincerely submitted to the judgment of more able and intelligent men. In national matters of this important concern, it would be presumption to suppose, that imagination may not have crept in with reason, or error with truth. Fallibility is the constant attendant upon human nature. The Author has taken pains carefully to collect the most known and approved facts, which relate to the subject. These will speak for themselves, when the opinions which he has formed upon them are forgotten, and in the duft.

F I N I S.

APPENDIX.

IT is to be hoped that Great Britain and America will speedily settle, by treaty, the commerce of the two countries, upon a satisfactory and solid foundation. The closer their union, the greater will be their mutual advantages. Upon this ground, and in this hope, the following plan of an act of parliament (when the several parts which relate to the duties, are properly investigated) is with deference offered to the Public.

CONTENTS OF THE BILL.

CLAUSE 1. NO goods to be imported, or exported, but in British-built ships, or in ships of the built of the United States, the property of British subjects, or the joint property of British subjects and the citizens of the United States; or in ships of the built of the United States, and the property of the citizens thereof.

2. Ships of the built of the United States, the property of British subjects, or the joint property of British subjects and the citizens of the United States, to be deemed British-built ships.

A

3. Such

3. Such ships, on reporting in Great Britain, to deliver a certificate of their built.

4. On their arrival in the West Indies, before they take in a loading for Great Britain, to produce the certificate of their built.

5. Such ships, on their arrival in Great Britain, to be registered.

6. Certificate of the register to be delivered to the master.

7. On the ship's name being changed, to be registered de novo.

8. On a certificate being lost, a new one to be granted.

9. Ships belonging to the United States to be subject only to the same port charges as British ships.

10. Any doubts arising of the built or property of ships of the United States, officers may examine.

11. The master, on reporting and clearing outwards, to give a true account of his ship and the goods on board. A proviso that no certificate, bond, &c. be required from ships of the United States.

12. Bond to be taken for all British ships, entering out for the United States, to return to Great Britain.

13. Goods of the growth, &c. of the United States, chargeable with duties, enumerated.

14. Goods of the growth, &c. of the United States, to be imported duty free, enumerated.

15. Goods for dyers use, though not of the growth, &c. of the United States, to be imported in their ships, chargeable with duties, enumerated.

16. Goods, though not of the growth, &c. of the United States, to be imported duty free in their ships, enumerated.

Goods

17. Goods of the growth, &c. of the United States, not enumerated, to be subject to the duties on similar goods.

18. All bounties formerly paid upon the importation of goods from the United States, to ceafe.

19. Goods of the growth, &c. of the United States, liable to duties, to be put into the king's warehoufes upon bond.

20. Not to be landed until due entry is made at the cuftom-houfe.

21. Importer may affix a lock to the warehoufe, which the officer is required to do, and to grant accefs, at all reafonable hours, to the importer, to examine and receive the goods, but not lefs than one package at a time.

22. Certificate of the duties being paid, or fatisfied, to be produced before delivery of the goods.

23. The duties not fatisfied within   months, commiffioners may direct the goods to be fold, to pay the charges.

24. Marks to be put upon each package, and the weight or gauge entered in books, kept for that purpofe.

Warehoufe-keeper to deliver in an account to the commiffioners every fix months.

Any goods delivered out before duties are paid, warehoufe-keeper to be rendered incapable and forfeit   pounds.

25. May be delivered out of the warehoufe for exportation, upon fecurity being given.

26. No tobacco to be imported in cafks under   lbs.

27. Indigo not to pay duty on exportation.

A 2   28. Bounties

28. Bounties to be granted on the exportation of gunpowder, fail cloth, filk, refined fugar, Britifh and Irifh linen.

29. Goods chargeable with duties on exportation, enumerated.

30. Foreign goods, exported to the United States, to be entitled to the fame drawback of duty, and fubjeƈt to the fame regulations, as if exported to foreign parts.

31. Goods, not enumerated, fubjeƈt to regulations on fimilar goods exported by Britifh fubjeƈts.

32. Ships of the built of the United States, the property of the citizens thereof, or qualified as Britifh fhips, may trade between the United States, and the plantations in America and the Weft Indies.

33. Goods of the growth, &c. of the United States, which may be imported into the plantations in America and the Weft Indies, enumerated.

34. Goods of the growth, &c. of the Plantations in that part of America called the Weft Indies, which may be exported to the United States, enumerated.

35 General claufe, fubjeƈting goods liable to duty to the regulations in ufe.

A

B I L L

FOR THE

*Eſtabliſhment and Regulation of the Trade be-
tween the Subjects of Great Britain, and the
Citizens of the United States of America.*

WHEREAS it is expedient to remove the obſtructions
which at preſent affect the trade carried on with the
United States of America, and to eſtabliſh the ſame
upon a ſolid and permanent foundation :

1. Be it enacted, &c. That no goods or commodities,
of the growth, production, or manufacture of Great
Britain, or of any land, iſland, plantation, or territory, which now, or ſhall hereafter, belong unto, or
be in the poſſeſſion of his majeſty, his heirs, and ſuc-
ceſſors, ſhall be exported to the United States of
America ;

No goods to
be imported, or
exported, but in
Britiſh - built
Ships ; or in
ſhips of the
built of theUni-
ted States, the
property of Bri-
tiſh ſubjects ; or

A 3

the joint proper-
ty of Britifh fub-
jeƈts, and the
citizens of thofe
States ; or in
fhips of the built
of the United
States, and the
property of the
citizens thereof.

America ; or any goods or commodities, of the growth
or produƈtion of the faid United States, or any of the
territories thereof, be imported into Great Britain, or
any land, ifland, plantation, or territory as aforefaid,
otherwife than in fuch fhip or fhips, veffel or veffels,
as are herein after defcribed—that is to fay—in fuch
fhips or veffels as do truly, and without fraud, belong
to the people of Great Britain, or any land, ifland,
plantation, or territory as aforefaid, as the proprietors
or right owners thereof according to law ; whereof the
mafter and three-fourths of the mariners are Britifh
fubjeƈts ; or in fuch fhips or veffels as are of the
built of the faid United States, and are the property
of Britifh fubjeƈts, or the joint property of Britifh fubjeƈts and citizens of the faid States, both in the manner and under the regulations herein after prefcribed
by this aƈt, and navigated as aforefaid ; or in fuch fhips
or veffels as do truly and without fraud belong to
the citizens, and are of the built of the faid United States; under the penalty of the forfeiture and
lofs of· all fuch goods and commodities, and of the
fhip or veffel in which they were imported or exported,
with all her guns, tackle, furniture, ammunition, and
apparel ; one moiety of the fame to the ufe of his
majefty, his heirs and fucceffors, the other moiety to
the ufe of fuch perfon or perfons as will feize on,
inform, or fue for the fame, or the value thereof; to
be fued for, levied, recovered, or mitigated, by fuch
means or methods, as any fine, penalty, or forfeiture
is, or may be recovered or mitigated, by any law or
laws relating to his majefty's revenue of excife or
cuftoms, or by any of them ; or by aƈtion of debt,
bill, plaint, or information in any of his majefty's
courts of record at Weltminfter for that part of Great
Britain

Britain called England; or the courts of Exchequer
at Edinburgh, for that part of Great Britain called
Scotland; any law, ftatute, or cuftom, to the contrary notwithftanding.

2. And be it enacted, &c. That any fhip or veffel,
built in any port or place within the faid United States,
belonging truly, and without fraud, to the citizens of the
fame, or to the people of Great Britain, or of any
land, ifland, plantation, or territory as aforefaid, or
being the joint property of Britifh fubjects and the
citizens of the faid States ; and making her firft voyage
from the place where fhe was built to Great Britain,
or from any of the ports within the faid United States
at which fhe fhall take in her lading of goods for the
fame, or which fhall proceed with her firft lading of
goods to any land, ifland, plantation, or territory as
aforefaid, in America or that part called the Weft-Indies, and on difcharging the fame fhall take in another
lading of goods, and fhall proceed with the fame directly
to Great Britain ; three-fourths of her mariners being,
at the time of taking in the faid laft-mentioned goods,
Britifh fubjects ; and alfo conforming to the feveral regulations prefcribed by this act, fhall from thence forward
be deemed and pafs as a fhip of the built of Great Britain,
or any of his majefty's dominions, and fhall be qualified
to trade from or in any part of the fame, any law,
ftatute, or cuftom to the contrary notwithftanding.

3. And be it enacted, &c. That the mafter of every
fuch fhip or veffel which fhall be built in any of the
faid United States, and to be deemed and pafs as aforefaid, fhall, upon her firft fetting out or being firft
navigated at fea, have or be furnifhed with a certificate
figned by the Britifh conful or vice-conful, refident
in the place or port in the faid United States, where

Ships of the built of the Uni-
ted States the property of Britifh fubjects, or
the joint proper-
ty of Britifh fub-
jects and the ci-
tizens, or how u-
nited &c. to
be deemed Bri-
tifh-built fhips.

Such fhips,
on reporting in
Great Britain, to
deliver a certifi-
cate of their
built.

the said ship or vessel was built ; and, if there be no
consul in the said port or place, to be signed by the
principal officer or officers of the customs thereof ;
or, for want of such officer, by the chief magistrate
of the said United States resident therein or the nearest
thereto ; describing the place where the same was built,
the burthen thereof, and the names of the owners,
whether British subjects, or citizens of the said United
States, to whom the same belongs ; which said certificate shall be produced by the said master on' reporting the same in Great Britain.

*On their arri-
val in the West
Indies, before
they take in a
loading for Great
Britain, to pro-
duce the certifi-
cate of their
built.*

4. And be it enacted, &c. That, on the arrival of
every such ship or vessel at any port in any land,
island, plantation, or territory as aforesaid, in America,
or that part called the West-Indies, from the place
in which she was built, or from the port in which
she took in her loading of goods for the same, the
aforesaid certificate shall be produced to the principal
officer or officers of his majesty's customs in the said
port, before she is permitted to take any goods on
board for Great Britain ; and after copies thereof are
taken (one of which shall be transmitted to the commissioners of his majesty's customs in Great Britain),
the said certificate shall be returned to the master.

*Such ships, on
their arrival in
Great Britain,
to be registered.*

5. And be it enacted, &c. That no such ship or vessel,
qualified as aforesaid, shall afterwards be deemed and
pass as a ship of the built of Great Britain, or any of
his majesty's dominions, unless the same, or one half
part thereof at the least, shall belong to, and whereof
the master and three-fourths of the mariners are
British subjects ; nor unless the British owners shall,
upon his or their oath before the principal officers of
the port at which the said ship or vessel shall arrive

from

from her firſt voyage, or in which he or they ſhall reſide, make proof thereof in the words following, deſcribing particularly the names, deſcriptions, and places of reſidence of the ſeveral owners, whether Britiſh ſubjects, or citizens of the ſaid United States : that is to ſay——" That the ſhip   of
" whereof   is at preſent maſter, being a
"   of   tons, was built at   within
" the territories of the United States of America, in
" the year   ; and that   of
" (is or) are at preſent (owner or) owners thereof ;
" and that no foreigner, or other perſon, has, directly
" or indirectly, any ſhare, part, or intereſt therein."

6. And be it enacted, &c. That ſuch oath, being atteſted by the cuſtom-houſe officer or officers who adminiſtered the ſame, under their hands and ſeals, ſhall, after having been regiſtered by them, be delivered to the maſter of the ſhip for the ſecurity of her navigation ; and a duplicate of the ſaid regiſter ſhall be immediately tranſmitted to the commiſſioners of his majeſty's cuſtoms in the port of London, in order to be entered in a general regiſter to be kept there for the purpoſe.

7. And be it enacted, &c. That no ſhip's name, regiſtered as aforeſaid, ſhall be afterwards changed without regiſtering ſuch ſhip de novo : which is alſo hereby required to be done upon any entire change of property, and delivering up the former certificate to be cancelled ; under the ſame penalties, and in the like method, as herein before directed ; and that in caſe there be any alteration of property by the ſale of one or more ſhares, in any ſhip after regiſtering thereof, ſuch ſale ſhall always be acknowledged by indorſement before

before two witneſſes ; in order to prove, that the entire
property of the ſaid ſhip belongs to ſome of the ſubjeɥts
of his majeſty, or of the citizens of the United States,
(one half part in all caſes to belong to Britiſh ſubjeɥts)
if any diſpute ariſes concerning the ſame.

On a certifi-
cate being loſt,
a new one to be
granted. 8. And be it enaɥted, &c. That if the certificate of any
regiſter as aforeſaid ſhall be loſt, the ſhip or veſſel may
be regiſtered de novo, upon the maſter or perſon, having
charge of the ſaid ſhip or veſſel, and one or more of the
owners thereof, making proof upon oath to the ſatis-
faɥtion of the commiſſioners of his majeſty's cuſtoms,
(in caſe the owner or owners, or any of them,
ſhall reſide in Great Britain, Guernſey, or Jerſey) or
of the governor or colleɥtor of the cuſtoms reſiding
in any of his majeſty's dominions in America, or that
part called the Weſt Indies (in caſe ſhe was regiſtered
in the ſame, and none of the owners ſhall reſide in
Great Britain, Guernſey, or Jerſey), of the loſs of
ſuch certificate, and likewiſe of the name, burthen,
built, property, and other particulars required by this
aɥt, in the ſame manner, and before the ſame perſons,
as required upon original regiſters ; and ſhall likewiſe
give good and ſufficient ſecurity, in the penalty of
500l. if the ſhip or veſſel be of the burthen of 100
tons, and ſo in proportion for every ſhip or veſſel of a
greater burthen, to the colleɥtor of the port to which
ſuch ſhip or veſſel ſhall belong, that the original cir-
tificate has not been, nor ſhall be fraudulently diſpoſed
of, or uſed, contrary to law ; and that the ſame, when
found, ſhall be delivered up to the commiſſioners of
the cuſtoms to be cancelled. In ſuch caſe it ſhall and
may be lawful for the commiſſioners of his majeſty's
cuſtoms, and the governor and colleɥtor of the
                                                cuſtoms

cuftoms refiding as aforefaid, and the faid commiffioners, governor, and collector, are hereby required
to permit the faid fhip or veffel to be regiftered de novo,
and the proper officers fhall deliver a certificate thereof
to the owner or owners, regiftering the fame in the manner directed by this act, and therein mention the name
by which the fhip or veffel was formerly regiftered; and
that fuch certificate of a new regifter is granted in pur-
fuance of this act, inftead of a former certificate, which
appears, by fuch proof as this act requires, to be loft;
and that fuch new regifter and certificate fhall have the
fame force and effect, as if the fame were an original regifter and certificate, and no other; and a duplicate thereof fhall be tranfmitted by the officers who fhall grant
the fame, to the commiffioners of his Majefty's cuftoms.

9. And be it enacted, &c. That every fhip or veffel
belonging truly and without fraud to the citizens, and
which is of the built of the faid United States, arriving
in the ports of Great Britain, or of any land, ifland,
plantation, or territory as aforefaid, fhall be fubject
only to the payment of fuch duties for lights, pierages,
and other port charges, as are now ufually paid by Britifh-built fhips, any law, ftatute, or cuftom to the contrary notwithftanding *.

*Ships belong-
ing to the citi-
zens of the
United States to
be fubject only
to fuch port
charges as Bri-
tifh-built fhips.*

10. And be it enacted, &c. That, in cafe any doubt
concerning the property of any fhip or veffel belonging
to the faid United States, or of the place from whence
fhe fhall come, fhall arife in Great Britain, or any land,
ifland, plantation, or territory as aforefaid, the princi-

*Any doubt a-
rifing of the
built or property
of fhips of the
United States,
officers may ex-
amine.*

---

* The very high port charges in Great Britain, and her Weft India
iflands, and the equally low port charges in France, and the French Weft
Indies, render this claufe neceffary, in order to encourage the Americans
to make this country an entrepot.

pal

pal officer or officers of the customs in the said port shall examine the bills of lading, and all other documents which may conduce to the ascertainment of the same; which said examination they are hereby directed and required to make, previous to the said ship or vessel being admitted to entry and to break bulk.

The master, on reporting and clearing outwards, to give in a true account of his ship and the goods on board her.

11. And be it enacted, &c. That the master of any ship or vessel belonging to the citizens, and of the built of the said United States, shall, without delay, on his arrival in any port of Great Britain, or in any land, island, plantation, or territory as aforesaid, and also on clearing out the same, make a just and true entry upon oath, of the burthen, contents, and loading of every such ship or vessel, with the particular marks, numbers, qualities, and contents of every parcel of goods therein laden, to the best of his knowledge; also where and in what port she took in her lading, and to what port she is bound; of what state built, how manned, the name of the master and owners during the voyage, inwards or outwards; and shall also conform to the several regulations prescribed by this act, and to the several laws and regulations now in force for the entry of ships from or to foreign ports not within the dominions of his Majesty, and not repealed or altered by the same.

No register, bond, &c. to be required from ships of the United States.

Provided always, that no register, bond, certificate, or any other paper than what is directed by this act, shall be required from any such ship or vessel, or for any goods on board the same, any law, statute, or custom to the contrary notwithstanding.

Bond to be taken for all British ships entering out for the United

12. And be it enacted, &c. That for every British ship or vessel, or any ship or vessel qualified and deemed to pass as such by this act, as shall enter and clear out of any

port

port in Great Britain, or any land, ifland, plantation, or territory as aforefaid, for any port or place in the faid United States, fufficient bond, with one furety, fhall be given to the principal officers of the cuftoms in fuch port or place, from whence the faid fhip or veffel fhall enter and clear out, to the value of 1000l. if of lefs burthen than 100 tons, and of 2000l. if of that or greater burthen ; the condition of which fhall be, that the faid fhip or veffel fhall proceed to the port or place for which fhe hath been entered and cleared out ; and in cafe fhe fhall load any goods or commodities at the faid, or any port or place in the faid United States, that the fame fhall be, by the faid fhip or veffel, brought to, unladen, and put on fhore, (the danger of the feas only excepted) as follows — that is to fay — if the faid goods or commodities are enumerated goods, permitted by this act to be carried from the faid United States to any land, ifland, plantation, or territory as aforefaid, in America, or that part called the Weft Indies, the fame fhall be landed in fome port thereof ; but if any other than the faid enumerated goods, the fame fhall be landed in fome port of Great Britain ; which faid bond fhall not be difcharged, until a certificate is produced, within eighteen months from the date of the faid bond, (the danger of the feas excepted) from the conful, officer, or chief magiftrate as aforefaid, in the port or place in the faid United States, in which the faid fhip or veffel has been loaded ; and in cafe the fame has been laden with enumerated goods, for any land, ifland, plantation, or territory as aforefaid, in America, or that part called the Weft Indies, a certificate, as aforefaid, muft likewife be produced of the principal officers of the cuftoms, that the fame has

States, to return to Great Britain.

been

been duly landed in fome port thereof; any law, ſtatute, or cuſtom, to the contrary notwithſtanding. †

Goods of the growth, &c. of the United States chargeable with duties, enumerated.

13. And be it enacted, &c. That the following enumerated goods, of the growth or production of the ſaid United States, the property of the citizens thereof, or of Britiſh ſubjects, brought directly from the port where the ſaid goods can only, or moſt uſually are firſt ſhipped for tranſportation, duly imported and entered according to law, ſhall be ſubject to the payment of the duties, and entitled to the receiving back the ſame, or part thereof, on exportation, as are annexed to each article, any law, ſtatute, or cuſtom, to the contrary notwithſtanding. *

---

† An objection may be made to this clauſe, leſt it ſhould prove the means of preventing our being the carriers of thoſe goods of the middle and ſouthern ſtates, which are not conſumed in Great Britain. But when it is conſidered, that theſe goods may be put in order for a market, upon more advantageous terms in this country, than in any other, and that it tends to promote the making Great Britain an entrepot; at the ſame time that it forwards a connection between the two countries; (independent of its other advantages) this objection will certainly be over-ruled.

---

* In order to form a judgment of the duties proper to be impoſed, and the drawbacks to be repaid, upon theſe articles, the former payments and repayments, incluſive of the additional duties during the war, are inſerted; (excepting hemp, iron, and aſhes, againſt which, leſt a difference ſhould give any umbrage to Ruſſia, the duties and drawbacks upon thoſe articles, when imported from the northern ſtates, are placed)—That the whole of the American trade may be taken into conſideration, and ſuch duties impoſed and drawbacks repaid, as ſhall be deemed, by perſons converſant in the trade, to be advantageous to us. Particular attention ſhould be paid to thoſe articles that are the ſtaple of any ſtate; ſuch as rice, which for want of conſumption, contributing little to the revenue, yet will contribute very largely to our navigation; beſides other great advantages in making this country an entrepot for it. Naval ſtores, being eſſentially neceſſary to our navigation, ſhould be imported duty free; and oil, as being uſeful to us in ſome of our manufactures, and of which our conſumption is very great for many purpoſes, ſhould be ſuffered to be imported upon payment of a moderate duty. Furs, and other articles, ought to be properly inveſtigated, that when an act is made, it may be as complete as poſſible,

Aſhes

	Duty to be paid on Importation.				Drawback to be repaid on Exportation.			
	£.	s.	d.	20th.	£.	s.	d.	20th.
Ashes vocat. Pot ashes, ... the cwt.		2	2	$\frac{8}{20}$				
Pearl ashes, ... ———		2	2	$\frac{8}{20}$				
Weed ashes, ... ———			6	$1\frac{1}{8}$				
Wood ashes, ... ———			6	$1\frac{12}{20}$				
Copper ore, ... ———			8	$\frac{5}{20}$			7	$1\frac{10}{20}$
Furs, vocat. Bear skins, black or red, . . the piece		5	6			5		
———, white, . . . ———		11				10		
Beaver skins, ... the whole piece			1	$\frac{2}{20}$				
——— wombs, . . . the piece			5	$\frac{10}{20}$		5		
Catskins, the hundred, containing 5 score		11				10		
Foxes, the black fox skin, ...	2	15			2	10		
———, the ordinary skin, ...			4	$\frac{8}{80}$			4	
Martrons or Martins, the timber, containing 40 skins, ...	2	15			2	10		
Minks tawed, the timber, containing 40 skins, ...	1	2			1	0	0	
——— untawed, ———		16	6			15		
Otter skins, ... the piece	1		4	$\frac{10}{20}$	1		3	
Wolf skins, tawed, . . ———		8	3			7	6	
——— untawed, . . . ———		6	3	$\frac{18}{20}$		5	9	
Wolverings, . . . ———		3	5	$\frac{5}{20}$		3	1	$\frac{10}{20}$
All other furs (except those rated among skins) for every 20s. of their real value, upon oath, . .		5	6			5		
And if any of the aforesaid furs, or any other furs, are tawed or dressed, and are not before charged as such, they are to pay more for every 20s. of their real value, upon oath,		6	7	$\frac{4}{20}$			7	$\frac{4}{20}$
Hemp, rough, ... the cwt.		3	8			3	4	
Hides, vocat. Buff hides, . . . the hide		4	4	$\frac{16}{20}$		4	1	$\frac{16}{20}$
and besides for every pound wt.			7	$\frac{14}{20}$			5	$\frac{7}{20}\,\frac{1}{3}$
Cow or horse hides in the hair, the piece			8	$\frac{5}{20}$			7	$\frac{10}{20}$
——— ——— tanned, ———		2	9			2	6	
and besides for every pound wt.			3	$\frac{17}{80}$			2	$\frac{11}{20}\,\frac{4}{8}$
Elk hides dressed or undressed; *vide* Skins								
All other hides, and pieces of hides, not before particularly charged, for every 20s. of their real value, upon oath		5	6			5		
And besides, if dressed in oil, the lb. wt.			7	$\frac{14}{20}$			5	$\frac{7}{20}\,\frac{1}{3}$
——— ——— tanned, ———			3	$\frac{17}{20}$			2	$\frac{11}{20}\,\frac{4}{8}$
——— ——— tawed, . . the hide		3	10	$\frac{4}{20}$		2	8	$\frac{4}{20}$
Horns of Cows or Oxen, the hundred, containing 5 score	1	10			1	8		
——— Harts or Stags, . . the hundred		6	7	$\frac{4}{20}$		5	10	$\frac{4}{20}$

Horn

	Duty to be paid on Importation.			Drawback to repaid on Exportation.		
	£	s.	d.20lb	£	s.	d.20
Horn Tips, the hundred, containing five score			$6\frac{13}{20}$			6
Iron unwrought, called bar-iron, . . the ton wt.	2	16	$1\frac{7}{20}$	2	12	$7\frac{2}{20}$
—— Ore, ...		2	9		2	6
—— called pig-iron, . . . ——		5	6		5	
Oil, vocat. Train oil or blubber, the ton, containing 252 gallons . . .		13	$2\frac{8}{20}$		10	$2\frac{8}{20}$
Pitch, small or great band, the last containing 12 barrels . . .		11			10	
Rice, ... the cwt		7	4		6	8
Rosin, ... ——		1	$5\frac{12}{20}$		1	$3\frac{12}{20}$
Sarsaparilla, ... the pound wt.			$8\frac{16}{20}$			$7\frac{16}{20}$
Saffafra, wood or roots, . . the cwt.		4	$4\frac{16}{20}$		3	$10\frac{16}{20}$
Snake root, ... the pound wt.			$9\frac{17}{20}\frac{14}{10}$			$8\frac{16}{20}$
Skins, vocat. Buck or deer skins, in the hair, the skin			$8\frac{5}{20}$			$7\frac{10}{20}$
—————— dressed ——————		1	$4\frac{10}{20}$		1	3
and besides for every pound wt.			$9\frac{18}{20}$			$\frac{13}{20}$
—————— Indian, half-dressed, the pound wt.			$4\frac{21}{20}\frac{1}{2}$			$3\frac{15}{20}$
Elk skins, dressed or undressed, the skin		1	$7\frac{16}{20}$		1	6
and besides, if dressed in oil, for every pound wt.			$7\frac{14}{20}$			$5\frac{7}{20}$
Fisher skins - - the piece		1	$7\frac{10}{20}$		1	6
Moose skins, - - ——		2	9		2	6
Musquash skins, - - the skin			$1\frac{13}{20}$			$1\frac{2}{20}$
Panther skins, - the piece		5	6		5	
Raccoons, - - the skin			$1\frac{13}{20}$			$1\frac{2}{20}$
Seal skins, - - ——			$5\frac{10}{20}$			5
and besides, if dressed, for every 20s. of their real value, upon oath,		6	$7\frac{4}{20}$			$7\frac{4}{20}$
and besides the aforesaid duties, if any of the aforesaid skins are tawed, tanned, or dressed, and not particularly charged as such, they are to pay for every 20s. of their real value, upon oath, - -		6	$7\frac{4}{20}$			$7\frac{4}{20}$
Tar, small or great band, the last containing 12 barrels		11			9	9
Tobacco, - - - the lb. wt.		1	$2\frac{19}{20}\frac{3}{4}$		1	$2\frac{19}{20}$
Turpentine common, - - the cwt.		2	$2\frac{8}{20}$		1	$11\frac{8}{20}$
Wax, - - - - ——		8	$9\frac{12}{20}$		7	$9\frac{12}{20}$
and besides, if bees wax ——		2	$2\frac{8}{20}$		2	$2\frac{8}{20}$
—— vocat. hard wax, - the lb. wt.			$8\frac{12}{20}$			$7\frac{16}{20}$
—— Bay or myrtle, - ——			$1\frac{13}{20}$			$1\frac{10}{20}$
Whalefins, - - the ton wt.	2	15	0	1	10	

14. And be it enacted, &c. That the following enumerated goods of the growth or production of the said United States, the property of the citizens thereof, or of British subjects, duly brought from the place of their growth, imported and entered as aforesaid, shall be imported into Great Britain free of duty, any law, statute, or custom to the contrary notwithstanding.

Goods of the growth, &c. of the United States to be imported duty free, enumerated.

Beaver wool
Flax, undressed or rough
Sago powder
Wood vocat. Anchor stocks
————————— Balks great, middle, and small
————————— Battens
————————— Battens 6½ inches wide or under
————————— Beach boards 2 inches thick or under
————————— Beach planks above 2 inches thick
————————— Beach quarters under 5 inches square
——————————————— 5 inches square and under 8 inches
Boards vocat. Barrel boards
——————————— Clap boards
——————————— Pipe boards or pipe bolts
——————————— Whiteboards for shoemakers
Boom spars
Cantspars
Capravens
Clapbolt or clapboards
Deals
——— of 20 feet in length, or under
Firewood
Fir quarters, under 5 inches square
——————— of 5 inches square, and under 8 inches
Handspikes
Headings for pipes, hogsheads, or barrels
Knees of oak for shipping, 8 inches square, and under
————————————— above 8 inches square
————————— small for wherries
Lath wood
Masts for ships, great, middle, and small
Oak boards
——————— under 2 inches thick, and under 15 feet long
——— Plank
——— Timber

B   Oars

Oars
Paling boards
Round wood
Scale boards
Spars, fmall
Spokes for cart wheels, long and fhort
Staves, vocat. Barrel ftaves
————————— Bow ftaves
————————— Kilderkin ftaves
————.————— Pipe and hogfhead ftaves
Wainfcot
——————— boards of all forts
Ufers, fingle, under 24 feet in length
——————— double, of 24 feet in length, and upwards
Wood for dyeing, of all forts
Walnut, or any fort of wood not rated

Goods for dyers ufe, though not of the growth, &c. of the United States to be imported in their fhips, chargeable with duties, enumerated.

15. And be it enacted, &c. That the following enumerated goods for dyers ufe, the property of Britifh fubjects, or of the Citizens of the faid United States, though not of the growth or production of the fame, imported into Great Britain in fhips or veffels Britifh-built, or qualified as fuch by this act, or in fhips or veffels belonging to the faid United States, duly imported and entered as aforefaid, fhall be fubject to the payment of the duties, and entitled to the receiving back the fame, or a part thereof, on exportation, as are annexed to each article, any law, ftatute, or cuftom to the contrary notwithftanding. *

* Thefe duties fhould be examined into. It is for the benefit of our manufactures that they fhould be brought in from all parts.

Alum

	Duty to be paid on importation.			Drawb repai port
	£.	s.	d.20th.	£. s.
Alum, — — — the cwt.	7	1	$1\frac{16}{20}$	6
—— ronifh or roach, —	1	5	$5\frac{11}{20}$	1
Alumen plume, — — the lb. wt.		2	$\frac{7}{20}\frac{3}{5}$	
Antimonium preparatum or ftibium,		1	$1\frac{1}{20}\frac{5}{5}$	
Britifh berries, for every 20s. value upon oath,	3	3	$3\frac{12}{20}$	2
Calabafha,	6	4	$4\frac{11}{20}\frac{1}{5}$	5
Caffina,				
Caffumber,	3	3	$3\frac{12}{20}$	2
Copperas, blue, — — the cwt.		10	$10\frac{11}{20}\frac{1}{5}$	
—— green, — —	1	7	$7\frac{16}{20}$	1
—— white, — —	2	11	$11\frac{4}{20}$	2
Grain or fcarlet powder, — the lb. cwt.		8	$8\frac{16}{20}$	
—— of fevil in berries —		4	$4\frac{8}{20}$	
Grana germanicum, for every 20s. value upon oath,	6	4	$4\frac{11}{20}\frac{1}{3}$	5
Grain of Portugal, or rotta, — the lb. cwt.		4	$4\frac{8}{20}$	
Gum arabic, — — —		6	$6\frac{12}{20}$	
—— Senegal, — — —	11			
—— lack, called cake lack, —		2	$\frac{7}{20}\frac{3}{5}$	
—— mount jack, for every 20s. value upon oath,	6	4	$4\frac{11}{20}\frac{1}{3}$	5
Jeffamin ointment,	6	4	$4\frac{11}{20}\frac{1}{5}$	5
Litharage of gold, — the cwt.		10	$10\frac{11}{20}\frac{1}{5}$	
——— filver		8	$8\frac{16}{20}$	
Oil of peony, for every 20s. value upon oath,	6	4	$4\frac{11}{20}\frac{1}{3}$	5
Pomatum,				
Platain,	3	3	$3\frac{12}{20}$	2
Salt petre, — — the cwt.	2	2	$2\frac{8}{20}$	1
Terra dulcis, for every 20s. value upon oath,	6	4	$4\frac{11}{20}$ 3	5
Weld, — — — the cwt.		9	$9\frac{18}{20}$	
Woad Ifland, or green woad, — the ton wt.	13			1 5
Verdigreafe, common, — the lb. wt.		3	$3\frac{6}{20}$	
——— chriftalifed, —	1	1	$1\frac{4}{20}$	

16. And be it enacted, &c. That the following
enumerated goods, the property of Britifh fubjects or
of the citizens of the faid United States, though not
of the growth or production of the fame, imported into
Great Britain in fhips or veffels Britifh built, or qualified
as fuch by this act, or in fhips or veffels belonging to
the faid United States, duly imported and entered as
aforefaid, fhall be imported into Great Britain free of
duty, any law, ftatute, or cuftom to the contrary notwithftanding.

Good
not o
growt
the U
States
portec
in the
enum

Aga-

Agarick - - - - ⎤
Annotto, - - - ⎥
Antimonium crudum, - - ⎥
Aqua fortis, - - - - ⎥
Archelia, or Spanish weed, - - ⎬ for Dyers use.
Argol, white and red, or powder, - ⎥
Arsenic, white or yellow, or rosalgar, ⎥
Bay berries, - - - ⎥
Brazil, or Fernambuc wood, - ⎥
Brazilletto, or Jamaica wood, - - ⎦
Box wood, - - - - - -
Cochineal of all forts, - - ⎫ for Dyers use.
Cream of tartar, - - - ⎭
Ebony wood, - - - - - -
Fustick, - - - ⎤
Galls, - - - ⎥
Gum stick lack - - - ⎬ for Dyers use.
Indigo, - - - ⎥
Indigo dust, - - - ⎥
Isinglass, - - - ⎦
Lignum vitæ, - - - - - -
Logwood, - - - ⎫ for Dyers use.
Litmus, - - - - ⎭
Madder, vocat. crop madder, and all ⎤
other bale madder, ⎬ for Dyers use.
———————— fat madder, - ⎥
——————————— mull madder, - ⎦
Madder roots, or rubia tinctorum, - for Dyers use.
Mahogany, - - - - - -
Nicaragua wood, - - - for Dyers use.
Olive wood, - - - - - -
Orchall, - ⎤
Orchelia. See Archelia, - ⎥
Pomegranate peels, - - ⎥
Red or Guinea wood, - ⎥
Safflore - - - ⎬ for Dyers use.
Sal armoniacum, - - ⎥
— gem, - - - ⎥
Sapan wood, - - - ⎥
Saunders, red or stock, - ⎦
Shumack, - - -
Stick lack. See Gum, - - - - -
Sweet wood, - - - - -
Tornsal, - - ⎫ for Dyers use.
Valonea, - - - ⎭

17. And be it enacted, &c. That all goods of the growth or production of the said United States, not enumerated, duly brought from the place of their growth, imported and entered, as aforesaid, shall be made liable only to the payment of such duties (if any) as are now paid, and shall receive such duties back, or a part thereof, on exportation to foreign parts, as are now received, and shall be otherwise subject to the regulations that similar goods, imported or exported by British subjects, in British-built ships, are subject to, any law, statute, or custom to the contrary notwithstanding.

Goods of the growth, &c. of the United Sta es not enumerated, to be subject to the duties on similar goods.

18. And be it enacted, &c. That all bounties which have hitherto been granted upon the importation of certain goods or commodities, the produce of the territories now composing the said United States, shall no longer continue to be paid, but from henceforth cease and determine, any law, statute, or custom to the contrary notwithstanding.

All bounties formerly paid upon the importation of goods from the United States, to cease,

19. And be it enacted, &c. That all such goods of the growth or production of the said United States, as shall be imported into Great Britain directly from the same, or any of them, upon the entry thereof at the custom-house, may forthwith, and before payment of all or any part of the duties, which such goods are charged with and liable to pay, be landed from on board the ship or vessel in which the same shall be so imported, and carried or put into such warehouse or warehouses, as shall be for that purpose provided, at the charge of the respective proprietor or proprietors, importer or importers of such goods, which shall be approved of by the commissioners of his majesty's customs or excise, or the major part of either of them

Goods of the growth, &c. of the United States liable to duties, to be put in the king's warehouse upon bond

B 3   for

for the time being, or by the principal officers of the
cuftoms or excife in the port in which the fame fhall
be landed ; upon the importer or importers aforefaid
firft giving, at his or their charge and expence, his or
their bond, or other good and fufficient fecurity, for
the full amount of all and every the duties which fuch
goods are charged with and liable to pay (which the
commiffioners or other proper officers of the cuftoms or
excife are hereby required and empowered to take)
payable as foon as the faid goods fhall be fold (provided
the fale of the fame fhall take place within   months
from and after the time they fhall be landed and put
into warehoufes as aforefaid). And if the faid goods
fhall not be fold or exported, in the manner and according to the regulations prefcribed by this act, within
the faid   months, then to pay the fame at the end
of fuch   months, fuch duty to be computed according to the weight or gauge of the faid goods, to
be taken at the time the fame fhall be fo landed, and
lodged in warehoufes as aforefaid.

20. And be it enacted, &c. That in cafe any fuch
goods fhall be landed, or put on fhore out of any fhip
or veffel, before due entry be made thereof at the
cuftom-houfe, and with the proper officers of the cuftoms or excife, at the port or place where the fame fhall
be imported, and the faid duties fecured ; or without a
warrant for the landing or delivering the fame, firft
figned by the proper officers of the cuftoms or excife ;
or without the prefence of a cuftom-houfe or excife
officer ; fuch imported goods as fhall be fo landed or
put on fhore, or taken out of any fhip or veffel contrary to the true meaning of this act, or the nature of
the fame, fhall be forfeited, and fhall or may be fued
for

Not to be
landed until due
entry is made at
the cuftom-
houfe.

for and recovered of the importer or proprietor thereof, in the manner and for the ufes as aforefaid.

21. And be it enacted, &c. That it fhall or may be
lawful for the proprietor or proprietors, importer or
importers of fuch goods, fo to be lodged in any fuch
warehoufe or warehoufes as aforefaid, to affix one lock
to every fuch warehoufe, the key of which fhall remain in the cuftody of fuch proprietor or importer ;
and to and for the proper officer or officers of the cuftoms or excife, appointed to attend fuch warehoufe or
warehoufes, to affix one other lock to the fame, the
key whereof to remain in the cuftody of the faid
officer or officers ; and the faid proprietor or proprietors,
importer or importers, fhall and may in the prefence
of the faid warehoufe-keeper or officer, (who are hereby required to attend at all reafonable times for that
purpofe) view, examine, open, feparate, garble, fhift,
weigh, and render merchantable, and fit for fale, the
faid goods or any part thereof, in the faid warehoufe
or warehoufes ; and fhall and may receive out of the
fame the faid goods or any part thereof, (but in no lefs
quantity than one cafk or package at a time) upon paying the faid duties for the fame, and upon producing
fuch certificate or receipt from the proper officers, of
the faid duties having been paid, in manner as is herein for that purpofe particularly prefcribed.

Importer may affix a lock to the warehoufe, which the officer is required to do, and to grant accefs at all reafonable hours to the importer to examine and receive the goods, not lefs than one package at a time.

22. And be it enacted, &c. That the faid goods fo
lodged in warehoufes as aforefaid, fhall or may from
time to time be delivered out of fuch warehoufe or
warehoufes refpectively, upon payment of his majefty's
duties thereon ; and upon the proprietor or importer,
or fuch perfon or perfons as fhall be appointed by him
or them for that purpofe, producing to the refpective

Certificate of the duties being paid or fatisfied, to be produced before delivery of the goods.

B 4 ware-

warehouſe-keeper or warehouſe-keepers, and the officers appointed to attend the ſaid warehouſe or warehouſes, a warrant or warrants, certificate or certificates,
ſigned by the proper officer of the cuſtoms or exciſe
appointed to receive the duties payable thereon, certi-
fying that he has received all and every the ſaid duties,
to which the ſaid goods, ſo deſired to be delivered out
of ſuch warehouſe, was liable and ſubject to pay, the
ſaid warehouſe-keeper or warehouſe-keepers and officers
attending ſuch warehouſe or warehouſes, ſhall deliver
ſuch goods as ſhall be mentioned or expreſſed in ſuch
warrant or warrants, certificate or certificates reſpective-
ly, to have paid or ſatisfied the ſaid duties.

The duties not ſatisfied within months, Commiſſioners of the Cuſtoms may direct the goods to be ſold to pay the charges.

23. And be it enacted, &c. That, in caſe ſuch
goods ſhall, after landed, remain in ſuch warehouſe or
warehouſes in which the ſame ſhall be ſo lodged for the
purpoſes aforeſaid, for any time exceeding the ſpace
of   months, after the ſame ſhall be ſo landed and
lodged in ſuch warehouſe or warehouſes as aforeſaid,
and the proprietor or importer, or other perſon or perſons by him or them appointed, ſhall not, within the
ſaid   months, pay or cauſe to be paid to the
proper officers appointed to receive the ſame, all and
every the duties to which the ſame are ſubject and liable
to pay, and ſhall omit to procure or bring ſuch certificate herein before directed to be had and made out,
from ſuch officers, to ſuch warehouſe-keeper or warehouſe-keepers, and to the officer or officers attending
the ſame, of the payment of the ſaid duties within the
time aforeſaid, that then it ſhall and may be lawful to
and for the ſaid commiſſioners of the cuſtoms or exciſe,
or the major part of either of them for the time being,
to direct and order ſuch goods, ſo lodged in ſuch warehouſe

houfe or warehoufes, for which the faid duties fhall not be paid within the time aforefaid, to be put up to fale by public auction, to the beft bidder or bidders for the fame, and the money arifing by fuch fale fhall be in the firft place applied, to the difcharge of the faid duties fo payable thereon, the charges attending fuch warehoufe or warehoufes, and the expence of fuch fale; and the furplus of the monies fo arifing by fuch fale (if any), after payment of the faid duties and charges, fhall go and be paid to the importer or proprietor of the faid goods, who fo landed and lodged the fame in the warehoufe or warehoufes as aforefaid.

24. And be it enacted, &c. That before fuch goods of the faid United States fhall be fo landed or lodged in fuch warehoufe or warehoufes, a mark fhall be fet on every cafk, veffel or package of the faid goods, mentioning the particular weight or quantity which is contained therein, according to the weight or gauge thereof to be then taken, and who is or are the refpective proprietor or proprietors, importer or importers thereof; and the keeper or keepers of fuch warehoufe or warehoufes, and the perfon or perfons who fhall be appointed by the commiffioners or proper officers of his majefty's cuftoms or excife to attend the faid refpective warehoufes, fhall each of them keep one or more book or books, wherein they fhall, refpectively and feparately, fairly enter in writing an exact particular and true account of all fuch goods of the faid United States, as fhall be brought into and carried out of the refpective warehoufe or warehoufes, to which he or they fhall refpectively belong; and the days and times when the fame

Marks to be put upon each package, and the weight or gauge entered in books kept for the purpofe.

same shall be brought in and carried out, and the name of the respective persons to whom, or for whose use, the same was delivered out; and shall, at the end of every six months or oftener, if required, transmit in writing an account thereof upon oath to the commissioners of the customs or excise for the time being, together with an exact account of the quantity then remaining in the respective warehouse or warehouses to which they respectively belong; and the commissioners of the customs or excise, as the case may be, are hereby required and enjoined, within one month after the same shall be respectively transmitted to them as aforesaid, to inspect and examine the said accounts; and if upon such examination it shall appear that any of the said goods were delivered out of the said warehouses, otherwise than is herein mentioned, or before payment of the duties, which such goods are charged with and liable to pay, for such the said goods, as shall have been delivered out of the said warehouses, then the said warehouse-keeper or warehouse-keepers, and officer or officers respectively offending therein, shall not only be disabled to hold or enjoy any public office or employment, but shall also forfeit and lose for every such offence the sum of   , to be sued for, levied and recovered, or mitigated by such ways and means and methods, as any fine, penalty, or forfeiture is or may be recovered or mitigated, by any law or laws as aforesaid, or by an action of debt, bill, plaint, or information in any of his majesty's courts as aforesaid.

Warehouse-keeper to deliver in an account to the commissioners every six months.

Any goods delivered out before duties be paid, warehouse-keeper to be rendered incapable and forfeit

25. And be it enacted, &c. That such part of the said goods as shall be intended for exportation to parts beyond the seas, shall be delivered out of such ware-

May be delivered out of the warehouse for exportation upon security being given.

varehouse or warehouses as aforesaid in the original
cask, bale or package only (or in some cask, bale or
package, containing the same quantity, in case the
original package be insufficient) unto the proprietor
or proprietors, importer or importers, or such buyers
or other persons, as the said proprietors or importers
shall have appointed in their behalf, upon sufficient
security to be given to his majesty, his heirs and suc-
cessors, (which security the commissioners of the customs or the time being, or the proper officer or officers of the customs, are hereby required and empowered to take) that the same and every part thereof
shall be exported to parts beyond the seas, and shall
not be re-landed in Great Britain, the Isle of Man,
or the Islands of Faro or Ferro; which said security
shall be discharged without fee or reward, by a certificate under the common seal of the chief magistrate
begonging to any place or places beyond the seas, or
under the hand and seal of the British consul, or of
two nown British merchants, then being at such place
or places, that such goods were there landed; or upon
proo made by credible persons, that such goods were
taken by enemies, or perished in the seas; the examination and proof thereof being left to the judgment of
the said commissioners of the customs for the time
being.

26. And be it enacted, &c. That no tobacco of the
growth or production of the said United States, shall be
brought or imported into Great Britain, otherwise
than in cask, case, or chest only, each cask, case, or
chest thereof containing   weight of neat tobacco at the least, under the penalty of the forfeiture

No tobacco to
be imported in
casks under
pounds.

ure of all the tobacco as fhall be imported contrary to this act, together with the cafks, cafes, or chefts, or other packages containing the fame.＊

Indigo not to pay duty on exportation.

27. And be it enacted, &c. That indigo of the growth, production, or manufacture of the faid United States, duly imported and entered as aforefaid, may be exported to any parts beyond the feas free of dity, any law, ftatute, or cuftom, to the contrary notwihftanding.†

Bounties to be granted on the exportation of gunpowder, fail cloth, filk, refined fugar, Britifh and Irifh linen.

28. And be it enacted, &c. That cordage, gunpwder, fail cloth, filk, refined fugar, and linen of Britifh manufacture, and Irifh linen, exported, under the rgulations required by law, to any part of the faid Lnited States, fhall be entitled to receive the following ounties on the fame:

CORDAGE made of hemp of foreign growth, or from hemp £. . d.
of the growth of Great Britain, Ireland, or of the growth of
the United States of America, the cwt.   — —   2   4¾
GUNPOWDER of the manufacture of Great Britain, exported
by way of merchandize, for every barrel the 100 pounds neat   4   6
SAIL CLOTH Britifh made, for every ell   ——   2

BRITISH MANUFACTURES OF SILK, videlicet,

Ribbands and ftuffs of filk only, the pound, avoirdupois wt. -   3
Silk and ribbands of filk, mixed with gold and filver, the
pound, avoirdupois weight   — — —   4

＊ It is an enquiry neceffary to male, whether it wd not be an advantage to increafe the weight from 450 pounds (undwhich it cannot be imported by the prefent laws) to the actual wet of a hogf-head of tobacco. It is generally underftood, that this ulation would be fatisfactory to the growers of this article.

† To encourage the States in which it is prodt to make this country an entrepot.

Silk

k ſtockings, ſilk gloves, ſilk fringes, ſilk laces, ſtitching or
ſewing ſilk, the pound, avoirdupois weight   —   —   1 $\frac{3}{8}$

uffs of ſilk and grogram yarn, the pound, avoirdupois wt.   -

uffs with ſilk mixed with inkle or cotton, the pound, avoirdupois weight   —   —   —   —   1

uffs of ſilk or worſted   —   —   —   —   6

SUGAR REFINED.

ugar refined in loaves compleat and whole, and in lumps
duly refined, for every Cwt.   —   —   —   1   6

————————called baſtards, ground or powdered ſugar, and
refined loaf ſugar broken in pieces, and all ſugar called
Candy, properly refined, for every cwt.   —   —   11 8

INEN made of Hemp or Flax in Great Britain or Ireland, or the Iſle of Man.

or every yard of the breadth of 25 inches, or more, and under the value of 5d. the yard   —   —   — $\frac{1}{2}$

———— ————value 5d. and under the value of 6d. the yard -   1

———— ————6d. and not exceeding 1s. 6d. the yard   —   1$\frac{1}{2}$

or every yard of Britiſh checked or ſtriped linen of the breadth
of 25 inches, or more, not exceeding 1s. 6d. and not under
7d. in value, the yard   —   —   — $\frac{1}{2}$

or every ſquare yard of diaper, huckaback, ſheeting, and
other ſpecies of linen, upwards of one yard Engliſh in
breadth, and not exceeding 1s. 6d. the ſquare yard in value   1$\frac{1}{2}$

or every yard of Britiſh and Iriſh buckrams and tilletings   — $\frac{1}{2}$

or every yard of Britiſh and Iriſh linen, and of Britiſh callicoes
and cottons, or cotton mixed with linen, printed, painted,
or ſtained in Great Britain, of the breadth of 25 inches, or
more, which before the printing, painting, or ſtaining
thereof, ſhall be under the value of 5d. the yard   — $\frac{1}{2}$

or every yard of the value of 5d. and under the value of 6d.
the yard   —   —   —   —   1

————————————— ———— ————6d. and not exceeding 1s. 6d.
the yard   —   —   —   —   1$\frac{1}{2}$

Goods chargeable with duties on exportation, enumerated.

29. And be it enacted, &c. That the following enumerated goods, the property of British subjects, or of the citizens of the said United States, duly exported and entered according to law, shall be subject to the payment of the duties that are annexed to each article, that is to say :*

Article		Duty to be paid on Exportation. £. s. d. 20th
Agarick, trimmed or pared, — —	foreign, the pound,	2 4/20
———— rough or untrimmed		1 1/20
Alum, — — —	British, the cwt.	1 1 4/20
Annotto, — — —	foreign, the pound	6 6/20
Antimonium Crudum, — — —		2 4/20
Aqua fortis, — — — the bottle containing 4 gallons		1 2 17/20
Argol, — — — the cwt.		7 14/20
Arsenick, — — — the pound		0 7/20 0 3
Bayberries, — — — the cwt.		1 9/20 1/2
Brazil or Fernambuc Wood, —		11 1 11/20
Brazilletto, or Jamaica wood,		7 3/20
Calve Skins, tanned, tawed, or dressed, —		1 1 4/20 6 12/20
Cards, vocat. Wool cards, vocat { new } not exceeding } the doz { old } 4 shillings the } pair in value }		3 19/20
Coals, ...		
Cochineal, foreign, . . . the pound wt.		2 4/20
Coney hair or wool, black or white, —		3 19/20
Copperas for every 20s. of the value, upon oath . .		1 1 4/20
Cream of Tartar, . . foreign, the cwt.		1 1 4/20
Fitches, the timber, containing 40 skins . . .		1 10
Fustick, ... foreign, the cwt.		1 1/20
Galls, . . . —		1 1 4/20
Glue, . . British, the cwt.		1 1
Gum Arabick, . . . foreign, the cwt.		1 13 3 1/20
——— Senegal, . . . —		5 9 6/20
Hair, vocat. hart's hair, — — the cwt.		1 9 1/20
Horse hair, —		6 7 4/20
Ox or cow hair, —		2 2 2/20
Hair of all other sorts, for every 20s. value, upon oath,		1 1 4/20

* These are the duties now paid, an examination into which is very necessary. Coals are not inserted, the difference in duty being so great between the exportation in British and foreign ships. They are left for consideration, but are of no consequence respecting the American trade.

Hares.

	£.	s.	d.	20th.

for every 20s. value, upon oath, — 1 1 4/20

es, or geldings — — each, — 5 6

— — — foreign, the cwt. — 11

inaris, for every 20s. value, upon oath, 3 3 12/20

d uncaft, the fodder, containing 20 cwt. 1 2

or every 20s. value, upon oath, 1 1 4/20

lead, — — — the cwt. 2 12/20 ½

ll forts, tanned, tawed, or dreffed, — 1 1 4/20

t. Cambrick or French lawns, the piece, 3 3 3/20

— — — — foreign, the cwt. 6 12/20

ll forts, — — 9 1 8/20

s, — 2 2/20 1 6/0

ood, — — — the ton wt. 4 4 12/20

— — — the cwt. 1 1 4/20

6 12/20

— — each, 1

Peels, — — foreign, the cwt. 4 16/20

ea. wood, 9 18/20

——the lb. wt. 6 6/20 1 6/0

ck, 3 2/20 3/0

1 7/20 1 5/0

foreign, the cwt. 6/20 3 6/20

0 16/20

0 8/20

Badger fkins, the piece 4 8/20

Beaver fkins, for every fkin or piece of fkin 1 11/20

——wool or wombs, the pound wt. avoirdupois 7 6/20

Cat fkins, the hundred 1 7 6/20

Coney fkins, black, with filver tails or without, the hundred, containing fix fcore 2 11 12/20

——grey ftag, the hundred, containing fix fcore 6 12/20

——feafoned, — 1 1 4/20

——tawed, — 8 16/20

——tawed and dyed into colours, the hundred containing 120 1 1 4/20

Dog fkins, the dozen 1 13/20

Elk fkins, the piece raw 1 1 4/20

Fox fkins, the piece 8/20 4/0

Hare fkins, 3 3/20 1 6/0

Kid fkins in the hair, the hundred, containing five fcore 6 12/20

——, dreffed 8 16/20

Lamb fkins vocat. mofe fkins { tawed with the wool, the hundred, containing fix fcore 11

untawed, — 11

Otter

	Duty to be paid on Importation.
	£. s. d.20th.
Otter skins, raw, ... the piece	13/20 1/3
tawed, ... ———	17/20 1/3
wombs, ... the mantle	6 1/20
Rabbit skins, black, ... the hundred	9 18/20
Sheep and { tawed with the wool, the hundred, containing six score	3 3 12/20
lamb skins { dressed without wool ——— ———	2 9
{ pelts, the hund. containing five score	3 8
Sheep skins, tanned, tawed, or dressed, . the cwt.	1 1 4/20
Squirrel skins, ... the thousand	2 9
Swan skins, ... - . the piece	1 13/20
Wolf skins tawed, ... ———	3 12/20 1/3
All other skins (except deer skins, native or foreign, dressed in oil in Great Britain) for every 20s. value, upon oath	1 1 4/20
Stick lack, ... foreign, the cwt.	2 2/20 7/16
Tin unwrought, ... the cwt.	3 3 12/20
Tornsal, ... - foreign, the cwt.	1 7/20 13/...
Valonea, ... ——— the ton wt	3 10 4/20
Verdigrease, ... ——— the pd. wt	3/20 2/3
Wool, vocat. cotton wool, of the British plantations, for every 20s. value, upon oath	1 1 4/20

Foreign goods exported to the United States, to be entitled to the same drawback of duty, and subject to the same regulations, as if exported to foreign parts.

30. And be it enacted, &c. That all goods of the growth, production, or manufacture of parts beyond the seas, which have been imported into Great Britain, whether entitled to draw back the whole, or any part of the duty paid on importation, or that have paid no duty inwards, or that the time allotted for drawing back the duty is elapsed, may be (except otherwise directed by this act) exported to the said United States, or the territories thereof, under the like regulations, and entitled to the same drawback of duty, as if the said goods were exported by British subjects to any foreign parts beyond the seas, otherwise than that all securities taken on the exportation thereof, and necessary to be discharged by certificate, shall be only done by certificate under the hand and seal of the British consul,

vice-

vice-conful, officers, or magiftrates, or on proof made of the faid goods being taken or perifhing in the feas, both in like manner as aforefaid, any law, ftatute, or cuftom to the contrary notwithftanding.

31. And be it enacted, &c. That all goods of the growth, production, or manufacture of Great Britain; not enumerated in, or otherwife directed by this act, may be exported to the faid United States, or the territories thereof, fubject to the fame regulations and reftrictions, as if exported by Britifh fubjects to any foreign parts beyond the feas, ctherwife than that all fecurities taken on the exportation thereof, fhall be difcharged by certificate as aforefaid, any law, ftatute, or cuftom to the contrary notwithftanding.

Goods not enumerated, fubject to regulations on fimilar goods exported by Britifh fubjects.

32. And be it enacted, &c. That every fhip or veffel belonging to the citizens, and which are of the built of the faid United States, or qualified as a Britifh fhip by this act, and conforming to the feveral regulations prefcribed by the fame, fhall be fuffered to enter into any land, ifland, plantation, or territory as aforefaid, in America, or the Bahama, or Bermuda, or Somer ifands, or that part called the Weft-Indies, any law, ftatute or cuftom to the contrary notwithftandingi

Ships of the built of the United States, the property of the citizens thereof, or qualified as Britifh fhips, may trade between the United States and the Britifh plantations in America or the Weft Indies.

33. And be it enacted, &c. That the following enumerated goods, of the growth or production of the faid United States, the property of the citizens thereof, or of Britifh fubjects, duly imported and entered according to law, may be imported into any land, ifland, plantation, or territory as aforefaid in America, or the Bahama or Bermuda, or Somer ifands, or that part called the Weft-Indies, fubject to the fame regu-

Goods of the growth, &c. of the United States which may be imported into the plantations in America and the Weft Indies enumerated.

lations

lations as British built ships, any law, statute, or custom to the contrary notwithstanding*.

Wheat.
Flour.
Barley.
Oats.
Rye.
Beans.
Pease.
Potatoes.
Rice.
Bread.
Biscuit.
Indian corn, and all other species of grain.
Fish.
Horses.
Mules.
Neat cattle.
Sheep.
Hogs.
Poultry, and all other species of live stock and live
    provisions.
Salt
Oil train, or blubber.
Pitch.
Tar.
Turpentine.
Hemp.
Flax.
Wood as aforesaid, wood for dying excepted.

---

* Some articles, fish in particular, may be objected to. But we should
consider, that an alteration in the whole system of our trade cannot be
made without risque; and that, if our own fisheries (supposing that they
are able in time to do it) can, at some distant period, fully supply our
West Indies, the planters will be great sufferers for the want of fish, till
that period arrives. It is most probable that it never will arrive. The
demand of the foreign markets for our fish has been generally equal to
the capacity of our fisheries to supply them; consequently, the advantageous situation of America threw the West India market chiefly into
the hands of her merchants; and they must in future possess it, as they
can supply it upon cheaper and better terms. The markets in Europe
are more adapted to the situation of this country; the fish ships, in their
circuitous voyage, making a freight home.

34. And be it enacted, &c. That the following enumerated goods of the growth or production of any land, island, plantation, or territory as aforesaid, in that part of America called the West-Indies, duly exported and entered according to law, may be exported under sufficient securities to be taken by the principal officers of His Majesty's Customs in the same, that the said goods shall be landed in the said United States; which security is to be discharged only by a certificate under the hand and seal of the British consul, vice-consul, officers, or magistrates, or on proof made of the said goods having been taken or perished in the seas, both in like manner as aforesaid, any law, statute, or custom to the contrary notwithstanding.

Goods of the growth, &c. of the plantations in that part of America called the West Indies, which may be exported to the United States, enumerated.

Sugar, vocat. brown sugars and muscovadoes,

————————white sugars,

————————pannells,

Melasses,

Rum,

Cocoa nuts,

Coffee,

Ginger,

Piemento,

Limes and oranges.

35. Provided always, and be it enacted, &c. That all and every such goods or commodities of the growth or production of the said United States, as shall be imported into Great Britain, or any land, island, plantation, or territory as aforesaid, and which shall either be lodged in warehouses as aforesaid, or otherwise; and all and every such goods or commodities of the growth, production, or manufacture of Great Britain, or any land,

General clause, subjecting goods liable to duty to the regulations in use.

land, ifland, territory or plantation as aforefaid, and which are refpectively fubject and liable to duties of excife and cuftoms on the importation or exportation thereof, fhall be fubject and liable to the fame; and to be applied to the fame ufes and purpofes, and to be managed and collected by the fame perfons, and in the fame manner, and to be fubject and liable to all and every the fame rules, entries, reftrictions, regulations, limitations, penalties, and forfeitures, as are in, and by this, or any other act of Parliament, by which the faid duties, or any of them are granted for fuch ufes or purpofes, particularly defcribed, appointed, limited, and enacted, fave and except in the particular inftances herein mentioned, and provided for, and to be applied to the fame.